PEE-WEE
HARRIS ADRIFT

PERCY KEESE FITZHUGH

Pee-Wee Harris Adrift

Percy Keese Fitzhugh

© 1st World Library, 2009
PO Box 2211
Fairfield, IA 52556
www.1stworldlibrary.com
First Edition

LCCN: 2009923481

Softcover ISBN: 978-1-4218-8867-5
Hardcover ISBN: 978-1-4218-8966-5
eBook ISBN: 978-1-4218-8768-5

Purchase *"Pee-Wee Harris Adrift"*
as a traditional bound book at:
www.1stWorldLibrary.com/purchase.asp?ISBN=978-1-4218-8867-5

1st World Library is a literary, educational organization
dedicated to:

- Creating a free internet library of downloadable ebooks

- Hosting writing competitions and offering book
  publishing scholarships.

1st World Library Literary Society

Giving Back to the World

"If you want to work on the core problem, it's early school literacy."

- James Barksdale, former CEO of Netscape

"No skill is more crucial to the future of a child, or to a democratic and prosperous society, than literacy."

- Los Angeles Times

"Literacy... means far more than learning how to read and write... The aim is to transmit... knowledge and promote social participation."

- UNESCO

"Literacy is not a luxury, it is a right and a responsibility. If our world is to meet the challenges of the twenty-first century we must harness the energy and creativity of all our citizens."

- President Bill Clinton

"Parents should be encouraged to read to their children, and teachers should be equipped with all available techniques for teaching literacy, so the varying needs and capacities of individual kids can be taken into account."

- Hugh Mackay

CONTENTS

CHAPTER I

ALONE

When Pee-wee Harris returned from Temple Camp in the fall, he found himself a scout without a patrol. He had indulged in a colossal speculation and lost out.

Forsaking the Raving Ravens, he had set forth to mobilize all the small, unattached boys at camp into the Pollywog Patrol, but the Pollywog Patrol had proved about as substantial as the shifting sand.

Like the beloved Black Lake it had both an inlet and an outlet. As fast as one boy entered it another had to go home, so that conducting the Pollywog Patrol was like pouring water into a leaky pail. Pee-wee, with all his flaunted efficiency, could not be at both ends of this patrol at the same time.

As soon as some miniature scout from New York had been duly initiated, some previously initiated scout from Chicago found that his time was up, and Pee-wee's time was chiefly occupied in rushing frantically about trying to keep pace with this epidemic of resignations.

At last the epidemic reached an acute stage and the

Pollywog Patrol, after a glorious career of nine days, was struck a mortal blow, never to be heard of again except in the pages of history. Its three remaining members were summoned to their several homes simultaneously; one new scout was hastily secured but on learning that he could not be patrol leader he tendered his resignation and was soon called home to attend his sister's wedding. Scout Harris faced a cruel world alone.

Meanwhile, Billy Simpson had been called to Temple Camp from Bridgeboro to fill (if anyone could fill) the enormous space left vacant in the Raven Patrol by the withdrawal of its enterprising genius.

"Never mind," said Mr. Ellsworth, the troop's scout-master, "there are plenty of fish in the sea—to say nothing of Pollywogs. Bridgeboro is full of permanent material. You have all this winter to round up a new patrol."

"Only don't round up any snow men because they melt," said Roy Blakeley, leader of the Silver Foxes; "and don't bother with shadows because you can't depend on them. And when you get a scout put a paper weight on him so he won't blow away."

"If you'll give me some of the biscuits you make, I'll use them for weights," Pee-wee shouted.

"You mean you'll eat them," Roy said. "What are you going to name the new patrol? Why don't you name it the Canned Salmon? Then they can't get away from you."

"Sure, you can have a can-opener for your emblem," said Dorry Benton.

"Maybe we'll call ourselves the Airedales because scouts

like fresh air," Pee-wee said. "I got a lot of ideas."

"He thinks Airedales are named after the air," said Doc Carson.

"Sure, just the same as Pennsylvania is named after the Pennsylvania Railroad," Roy said.

"You make me tired!" Pee-wee shouted disgustedly. "You leave it to me, I'll think up a name. I know four fellers already that'll join. Maybe I'll decide to start a whole new troop and not bother with this one."

"Why don't you start a whole new scout movement?" Roy asked. "Call it the Boy Scouts of Pee-wee Harris. Discharge the Boy Scouts of America altogether."

"I'll start something all right, you leave it to me," Pee-wee announced darkly. "You think you're smart just because you write stories about your adventures and you always make out that you're the hero. You always make out that I get the worst of it. Gee whiz, if I ever write any stories, I'll get my just deserts."

"Did I ever say you didn't get plenty of desserts?" Roy shot back at him. "I gave you three helpings in every story and that's all the thanks I get. You think so much about desserts that you're going to desert the troop. We should worry."

"If I write any stories I'll write them good and loud," Pee-wee shouted.

"Open the cut-out of your fountain pen," Roy said, "and be sure to turn to the right whenever you come to the end of a page and look out you don't skid."

"Maybe I'll write my remittances," Pee-wee said darkly.

"He means his reminiscences," said Arrie Van Arlen.

"I think," said Mr. Ellsworth, "that Scout Harris will be quite busy enough forming the new patrol, and when it is formed I hope he will present it to the First Bridgeboro Troop, B. S. A."

"That's us," said Westy Martin.

"I don't see how Pee-wee can get out of the troop," Mr. Ellsworth laughed, "because strictly speaking, he has never been in the troop; on the contrary the troop has been in him, as one might say."

"*Good night*, did he swallow that too?" said Roy. And he rolled backward off the troop-room table on which he had been sitting.

CHAPTER II

SATURDAY MORNING

Though Pee-wee was without a patrol he was by no means without a troop. He still held his position of troop mascot and official target for the mirthful Silver Foxes. He was a whole patrol in himself and held his own against raillery and banter, his stock of retaliatory ammunition seeming never to be exhausted.

"I can handle them with both hands tied behind my back," he boasted, which is readily enough believed since it was mainly his tongue that he used.

But recruits did not flock to Pee-wee's standard. Perhaps this was partly because of the fall and winter season when the lure of camping and roughing it was in abeyance. Perhaps it was because he was so small that boys were fain to think that scouting was a thing for children and beneath their dignity.

Once or twice during the winter, Pee-wee piloted some half-convinced and bashful subject to the troop-room, which was an old railroad car (of fond memory) down by the river. Here, in the cosy warmth of the old cylinder stove, the troop played checkers and read and jollied

Pee-wee, which was about all there was to do on winter nights. The visitors, unimpressed with these makeshift diversions of the off season, did not return, and so the good old springtime found Pee-wee still a scout indeed (with something left over) but a scout without a patrol.

And now the sturdy little missionary began to feel this keenly. Patrol spirit is usually not much in evidence during the winter; the several divisions of a troop intermingle and form a sort of club in which an odd member is quite at home. But with the coming of spring the patrol spirit becomes aroused. It is a case of "united we stand, divided we sprawl," as Roy Blakeley was fond of saying. Each patrol goes separately about its preparations for camping and hiking, does its shopping, repairs its tents, denounces and ridicules its associate patrols, and troop unity gives way somewhat to patrol unity. This is well and as it should be.

It was very much so with the well organized Bridgeboro troop. With the first breath of spring the Ravens became Ravens, the Elks foregathered and were Elks and nothing else, and the Silver Foxes began a series of exclusive meetings at Camp Solitaire under a big shady elm on Roy's lawn.

The Silver Foxes, imbibing the mirthful spirit of their leader, were all pretty much alike, and the Ravens were thankful that they were not like them, and the Elks congratulated themselves that they had more pep than the Ravens. "The Elks say the Ravens are no good and the Ravens say the Elks are no good and they're both right; we should worry," said Roy. "There's one good thing about the Elks and that is that they're not Ravens, and there's one good thing about the Ravens and that is that they're not Elks. They both have everything to be thankful for if not more so. They're in luck."

"Do you call that logic?" Pee-wee demanded in the tones of an earthquake. "If one thing is better than another thing how can that other thing be better than the other thing? You're crazy!"

"Goodness gracious, look who's here?" said Hunt Manners, who was sorting out some fish-hooks. "The whole Canned Salmon Patrol."

Pee-wee stood outside the tent, breathing hard after his long tramp up the hill to the Blakeley place.

"Don't you know this is private land?" Warde Hollister said, rather heedless of the possible effect of his remark.

"I didn't come in the tent, did I?" Pee-wee retorted wistfully.

"Come ahead in, Kid," said Roy. "Are you hungry? Here's some fish-hooks."

"No, I'm not hungry," Pee-wee said. He had been so touched by Warde's thoughtless remark that he held himself aloof from Roy's hospitality. "I only came up to tell you that the thunderstorm up the river did a lot of damage; a house was struck by lightning in North Bridgeboro and a lot of trees were blown down." This was not what he had come up for, though indeed the news was true, but his pride was touched by that remark of Warde's and he would not now admit that he had tramped up there just to visit them.

"Gee whiz, do you think I don't know that eight's a company, nine's a crowd with patrols?" he said. "Do you think I don't know that? Anyway, if I wanted to go and hang out with any patrol I'd go with the Ravens, wouldn't I? I only came up to tell you that, because I thought you'd like to know. Do you think I'm trying to find out your secrets? Gee whiz!"

"Come ahead in, Kid," said Roy; "Warde didn't mean that."

"I will not."

"What's the matter with you anyway?" Will Dawson asked.

"I'm not in your patrol," Pee-wee said.

"What's the big idea?" Westy Martin asked. "You weren't in it when you went on the bee-line hike with us either, were you?"

"That's different," Pee-wee said. "Anyway I was a scout then, because I was in the Ravens and anyway I've got to go to the store."

Before they realized it he was gone.

"What the dickens did you want to say that for?" Roy asked Warde.

"Oh, it just jumped out of my mouth," Warde said; "I didn't think he'd be so touchy. Wait, I'll call him back."

But the sturdy little figure trudging down the hill paid no attention to Warde's call. And the Silver Foxes, friendly and sympathetic as they were, were too preoccupied to think much about this trifling affair. Perhaps they had just a little disinclination to having visitors, even the little mascot, participating in their private councils just then.

The point of the whole matter was that Pee-wee had been unintentionally eliminated; it was a sort of automatic process attributable to the springtime. And he found himself alone. He was not out of the troop, but he was not in any of the patrols, and in spite of all his spectacular missionary work he had not been able to form a patrol.

Pee-wee's pride was as great as his voice and his appetite, and he would not sponge on the patrols which had a full membership and were busy with their own concerns. The rock on which he had stood all winter had split in three and there was no place for him on any of the pieces.

On Saturday morning the Silver Foxes went into the city to buy some camping things and to see a movie show in the afternoon. The Ravens went off for a hike. A Saturday spent alone was more than the soul of Pee-wee could endure, so he conquered his foolish pride and went up to Connie Bennett's house to find out what the Elks were going to do. He would not join in with the Elks, he told himself, but he would pal with any single Elk, or even with two or three. That would be all right as long as he did not foist himself upon a whole patrol. "Eight's a company, nine's a crowd, gee whiz, I have to admit that," he said to himself. "It's all right for me to go with one feller even if he's a scout but a patrol's different."

It was a wistful and rather pathetic little figure that Mrs. Bennett discovered upon the porch.

"Connie? Oh gracious, he's been gone an hour, dear," she said. "They all went away with Mr. Collins in his auto. I told him he must be back for supper. How is it you're not with them, Walter?"

"I—I ain't in that patrol," said Pee-wee; "it goes by patrols. Anyway I'm sorry I troubled you."

He turned and went down the steps and picking up a stick drew it across the slats of a fence as he went up the street. The outlandish noise seemed to act as a balm to his disappointment and to keep him company.

CHAPTER III

CASTLES IN THE AIR

The lonesomeness of Robinson Crusoe on his desert island was nothing compared to the lonesomeness of Pee-wee on that Saturday morning. He might have attached himself to any of the three patrols and had a day's pleasure, but his pride had stood in the way.

He had always been something of a free lance in the troop and been regarded as a troop institution. But there had always been his official place among the Ravens waiting for him whenever it suited his wanton fancy to return like a prodigal to the fold. Now, in the pleasant springtime with the troop divided for the summer rivalries, he found himself quite isolated.

No one was to blame for this; a scout must be in one patrol or another, and if all patrols are full then he must make himself the nucleus of a new one. That is what Mr. Ellsworth had told Pee-wee.

"Gee whiz, nucleuses aren't so easy to be, that's one thing," Pee-wee muttered to himself as he bent his aimless way in the direction of Barrel Alley. "Maybe he thinks it's easy to be a nucleus. Nucleuses are hard to be, I'll tell the world. Anyway I can be a pioneer scout, that's one thing. You don't have to be a nucleus or anything to be one of those. They don't have to bother with patrols, they don't, they're lucky."

He ambled along kicking a stone before him in a disconsolate, disgruntled way. He followed it wherever it went, ever and again kicking it back onto the sidewalk; the simple pastime seemed to afford him infinite relief. And meanwhile, glowing visions arose in his mind, such visions as no one but a poet or a lonely boy on a Saturday morning in the springtime could possibly have.

No one had injured him in the least, he was liked by all, he was simply the unhappy victim of circumstances. But in a mood of heroic retaliation against the troop he pictured himself as a pioneer scout residing aloof in a grim tower, surrounded by wireless apparatus and covered with merit badges. Scouts from all over the world would make pilgrimages to his obscure retreat for a timid glimpse of the mysterious hero.

The glowing vision was somewhat marred by his conception of himself eating a huge sandwich as he looked down from his parapet upon the worshipping throng below. Roy Blakeley would be down there among the others, his jollying propensity subdued by a feeling of awe as he gazed at the great scout hermit, the famous pioneer scout who sent messages to lesser scouts the world over. They would whisper, "he looks just like his pictures in *Boys' Life*," and he would smile down on them and…

Plunk! The pioneer scout had collided with a man on the sidewalk and he returned to Bridgeboro with a suddenness that surprised even himself.

Percy Keese Fitzhugh

"Excuse me," he said.

"Certainly," said the man.

Pee-wee recovered his rock, and began kicking it along the sidewalk again. "I'll show them," he said moodily.

He was about to ascend his scout throne again and engage in the gracious pastime of receiving delegations of common, ordinary scouts in his dim, wooded domain when he found himself at the edge of a region which was not in the least like the romantic wilderness of his vision. This was Barrel Alley, the habitat of Jimmy Mattenburg and Sweet Caporal and the McNulty twins.

Barrel Alley was the slum neighborhood of Bridgeboro and it was not very large. But it was large enough. Pee-wee explored the crooked, muddy, sordid street, gazing wistfully here and there for possible recruits. But no human material was to be seen. The older boys were playing craps in Dennahan's lot and the smaller boys were watching them. One lonely sentinel was perched on the fence scanning the horizon for cops. For this he received the regular union pay of a stale apple-core.

He was an unkempt urchin with an aggressive and challenging countenance, but he had solved several problems in economy. One of these was the entire elimination of stockings and garters. This was accomplished by the use of a pair of trousers with legs of such ample diameter and of such length as to render stockings altogether superfluous. This released both garters for more important duties, they being tied end to end, thus constituting a sort of single strand suspender which at its junction with his trousers in front was securely held by a large nail. His hair presented an appearance not unlike the negligent architecture of an eagle's nest, which is of the bungalow type in its loose irregularity. He had not the slightest reason for supposing that Pee-wee was equipped with commissary stores, but on general principles he said,

"Give us a hunk of candy, will yer?"

As luck would have it, this random shot, fired at every strange boy from the upper world, hit the mark, to his unspeakable astonishment. Pulling out of his pocket a licorice jaw-breaker of vast dimensions, Pee-wee sent it shooting in a bee-line at the face of the stranger.

Never before in all his checkered history had Keekie Joe ever received any edible of any character whatever in response to his menacing demands. He had always assumed that boys who were well dressed had fruit or candy in their pockets. He had sometimes required them to verify their denials by an exhibition of the interior of these receptacles. His invariable demand had become a habit with him. Therefore the little sugared black brick which now hit him in the eye came as an unprecedented surprise. For a moment he did not know whether to construe it as a propitiatory gift or a warlike missile.

"What's the matter with you, can't you catch?" Pee-wee demanded.

CHAPTER IV

KEEKIE JOE

It required but a few seconds for Keekie Joe to decide to run true to form. The situation was an unusual one, the missile was a delicious morsel, and was nothing more nor less than what he had demanded. But still it had been thrown at him and Keekie Joe elected to consider it as a shot fired by the enemy.

"Whatcher chuckin' things at me fer?" he demanded, descending from the fence and approaching Pee-wee with a terrible look of menace. He had been careful, however, to pick the jawbreaker up and put it in his mouth.

"Didn't you say you wanted one?" Pee-wee asked. "Didn't you just put it in your mouth?"

"Never you mind wot I done," said Keekie Joe. "D'yer think yer cin sass me?"

"I'll show you how to catch if you'll say you'll be a scout," Pee-wee answered. There could be no better illustration of his desperation as a scout missionary than this artless proposition to the sentinel of Barrel Alley.

"Who can't catch?" Keekie Joe demanded.

"You can't."

"Me?"

"Yes, you."

"Yer dasn' say it again."

"You can't catch, you can't catch, you can't catch," said Pee-wee.

There seemed nothing left now but to break off diplomatic relations altogether. The issue was clear. But Keekie Joe did not plunge his outlandish person into war.

"If I didn' have ter lay keekie I'd slam yer one," he announced.

"What's the use of giving you candy if we can't be friends?" Pee-wee said. "Gee whiz, I wouldn't care how much candy fellers threw at me; the more the merrier. They can throw mince pies at me for all I care," he added. "If you want to be a scout I'll show you how and we can start a patrol maybe."

The word patrol seemed to suggest something ominous to Keekie Joe, for he glanced furtively up and down the alley, and then waved his hand reassuringly to the group in the middle of the field.

Pee-wee perceived now that the scene of the crap game had been selected with keen military wisdom, affording a safe avenue of precipitate retreat in any direction. Disaster could have resulted only from a surrounding host. Officer

McMahon, the tyrant on this squalid beat, was large. But he was not large enough to surround the camp.

The crap-shooters of Barrel Alley had been surprised in every nook and corner of their neighborhood until they had hit upon the bold expedient of playing in an open lot, reposing their trust in a sentinel. It would not have been well for the sentinel to relax his vigilance.

"What I want ter join them scout kids fer?" Keekie Joe inquired. "Der yer call me a sissy?"

"Do you call the scouts sissies?" Pee-wee inquired angrily. "They have more fun than you do, that's one sure thing. If you don't want to join you don't have to but you don't have to get mad about it. Gee whiz, you're always mad, kind of. I guess you got up out of the wrong side of the bed, that's what *I* think."

This was not true, for indeed Keekie Joe did not sleep in a bed at all; he slept on a heap of old inner tubes in Ike Levine's tire repair shop. He was about to resent this slander from Pee-wee with a glowering look and a threat, when suddenly something happened, which precipitately terminated his performance of his official functions. His father called him from a tenement across the street, accompanying his summons with such dismal predictions of what would happen if he did not obey that the official sentinel had no choice but to desert his post.

"If I have ter come over there'n git yer," the father said, "I'll—"

Poor Joe glanced at his father in the window, then at the gamesters in the field. It was evident that chastisement of the severest character awaited him in any case. For a moment he had a wild notion of making a spectacular retreat along the street, crawling through a broken part of the fence beyond the range of parental vision, and resuming his duties of sentinel at another vantage point. Such a maneuver would at least postpone a reckoning with his father and enable him to be faithful to his trust. A very unworthy trust it may have been but his one thought was to be faithful to it. And there you have Keekie Joe in a nutshell...

CHAPTER V

A QUESTION OF DUTY

Pee-wee's advice to Joe in this predicament was rather singular, and the scout law on which he based it covered a rather larger field of obligation than was necessary in the circumstances.

"Go ahead over," he whispered; "you have to obey your parents and all other duly constituted authorities. I'll lay keekie for you while you're gone; go ahead over, I'll keep watch."

"Yes, you will!" said Joe incredulously. "I know youz guys, y'll put one over, that's what y'll do. Wat'd'yer mean, constute—con—authorities? Yes yer will, *not!*"

"That shows how much you know about scouts," Pee-wee said, always ready to explain the ins and outs of scouting. "Do you think I'd cheat? Gee whiz, I've got to be faithful to a trust, haven't I? If I say I'll do a thing I'll do it. You go ahead over and I'll keep watch and if I don't do it you can punch me in the eye the next time you see me."

It was not so much this proffer of indemnity as a supplementary threat from the window across the way which decided Keekie Joe. He did not believe in Pee-wee for he did not believe in anybody. But he was a bit puzzled at this self-possessed little stranger from another world. There was a straightforward, clear look in the little scout's eyes which bespoke both friendliness and sincerity and Keekie Joe did not understand this. The emergency decided him to repose faith in the strange boy but it was not in him to do this graciously.

"You keep yer eyes peeled till I git back, and giv'm the high sign, d'yer hear?" he said with insolent skepticism, "or the first time I see yer on Main Street I'll black up both yer eyes fer yer, d'yer see?"

"That's one thing I like about you," said Pee-wee; "gee whiz, you obey scout laws without even knowing them. That shows you're a kind of a scout and you don't know it."

Keekie Joe did not look much like a scout, as he shuffled across the street; he did not even look like the rawest of raw scout material. But statues are carved out of hard rock. And Keekie Joe was a very hard rock indeed.

Pee-wee vaulted up onto the ramshackle fence, placed one of those granite bricks known as a licorice jaw-breaker in his mouth, and prepared for his indefinite vigil. He was not thinking of the "constituted authorities," he was not thinking of the crap-shooters either; his back was turned to them and his all seeing eye was fixed on the distant street corner. He was thinking of Keekie Joe and of how Keekie Joe had tried to obey one of the good scout laws by being faithful to a trust. And there you have Pee-wee Harris in a nut-shell…

The game in the middle of the large field must have

become exciting, for its votaries were gathered into a close group. None of the players seemed able now to spare so much as a cautious glance toward the street. Once, during his intense preoccupation, Slats Corbett gave a quick, furtive glance afar, but it was only in a sort of sub-consciousness that he glimpsed a figure sitting on the fence, its back toward him. That was enough.

The group gathered closer, voices were heard in excited altercation, there were long intervals of silence. The group had shrunken and become compact. All were stooping. Their preoccupation seemed intense. They had forgotten all about the lookout. Occasionally some civilian passed along the distant alley and guilty instinct caused one or another of the group to glance thither to give a hasty appraisal of his mission and character. And so the wicked game went on. And the sports of Barrel Alley never knew that their stronghold had been invaded by the boy scouts.

Then around the distant corner appeared two figures in civilian clothes, strangers in Barrel Alley. They were County Detectives Slippett and Spotson. They strolled down the alley innocently. Keekie Joe, whose activities were chiefly local, knew them not. But Pee-wee Harris, Scout, knew them. On one of his long hikes he had seen them arrest a motorist in Northvale. He had seen them loitering in the post office at Little Valley.

They did duty in the various municipalities of the county where the familiar faces of the local officials were a stumbling block to the apprehension of wrongdoers. They were going to break up this ring of gambling rowdies, and so forth and so forth and so forth...

Pee-wee's first impulse was to shout, but on second thought it occurred to him that the army of invasion consisting of two, one of them might make a flank move on hearing his warning voice, and that one detective could thus drive the criminals into the very arms of the other, as they passed through the back yard of Chin Foo's laundry. Chin Foo's back yard was a sort of trap.

So instead of shouting he descended from the fence with lightning agility and ran across the field as fast as his legs would carry him, and pell-mell into the group.

"Two detectives are coming down the alley," he panted. "Beat it over that way and then you'll *sure* not run into one of them because they've got—got—a lot of strat—strat—strat—strat—egy—they have—you'd better hurry up."

The time it required for the group to disperse can not be indicated by any word in the English language. They were there and then they were not there. As Pee-wee stood amid scattered coins and dice he was conscious of distant forms scaling fences, wriggling through holes, and of one pair of legs disappearing majestically over a dilapidated roof. As a disorderly retreat it was a masterpiece.

It was not in Pee-wee's nature to run from anything or anybody. So there he stood amid the telltale mementoes of the dreadful game while Detectives Slippett and Spotson strolled into the field. They were just in time to behold a fleeting vision of forms wriggling through fences, gliding around buildings, and scrambling over roof tops.

County Detective Spotson was quick to sense the situation. Taking Pee-wee roughly by the shoulder he demanded in that sophisticated voice and manner which all detectives acquire and which sometimes passes for shrewdness, "What's the big idea, huh? Tipped them on, did you? Well, you're a very clever kid, ain't you?" He removed his big hand from Pee-wee's shoulder and injected his fingers down the back of the boy's neck, grabbing him by the collar and gathering it so that it almost choked him.

This terrifying grip, which is always intended to be considered as the preliminary of arrest, did not frighten Pee-wee as it would have frightened Keekie Joe, but it touched his pride and enraged him, and he wriggled frantically. There is no indignity which can be put upon a boy like this bullying, official grip of his collar.

"You let me go," he said excitedly; "I wasn't playing here and you didn't see me do anything wrong; you let me go, do you hear!" His utter helplessness, despite every contortion, to free himself from this degrading kind of grasp, drove him distracted and he kicked with all his might and main. "*You let me go, do you hear!*" he shouted.

"Well, what were you doing here then, huh?" the officer asked gruffly. "Yer gave'm the tip, didn't yer?"

"You let go, I'm not going to run away," Pee-wee said. "Do you think I'm scared of you? You let me go!"

"Do yer know what an accessory is?" Detective Spotson demanded, loosening his grip somewhat.

"It's something you buy to put on an automobile," Pee-wee said. "You let go, I'm not going to run."

Detective Spotson, like Keekie Joe, trusted nobody. But since he had no intention of arresting Pee-wee and since the diminutive captive seemed rather angered than frightened, he released his hold. By a series of wriggles and contortions, Pee-wee adjusted his clothing and settled his neck in his stretched neckband. "Why don't—why— why don't you take a—a—a feller your size?" he half cried and half panted.

The officers now began to have some glimmerings of the fact that here was a boy who did not belong in Barrel Alley. They were a little taken aback by the exhibition of so much pride and spirit. The customary, ominous grip of the collar had not worked.

"What were you doing down here, Sonny?" Detective Slippett asked.

"I came down to hunt for fellers to start a scout patrol," Pee-wee said, "and one feller was laying keekie for cops and he had to go home so I took his place, because he had to keep his word with those fellers, didn't he? Maybe you wouldn't promise fellers to do that but, gee whiz, if you did promise them you'd have to keep your word, wouldn't you? If he sees I help him maybe he'll get to be a scout, won't he? Do you mean to tell me it isn't more important to be a scout than it is to let fellers get to be arrested? Even—even Roosevelt said the scouts were important, but he didn't say it was important you should catch fellers, did he?"

"That's some argument," Detective Slippett said, half smiling.

"I know even better arguments than that," Pee-wee boasted.

"Well," said Detective Spotson rather more gruffly, "you'd better look out how you try to interfere with the law, young feller, 'cause first thing you know you'll find yourself in jail. And you'd better keep away from this outfit down here, too. Now you chase yourself back to where you belong—see?"

"You thought you were going to scare me, didn't you?" Pee-wee said.

CHAPTER VI

THE MISSIONARY

Pee-wee retraced his steps back across the field feeling righteous and triumphant. To him the interests of the Boy Scouts of America superseded every other interest and like the true missionary he did not scruple overmuch as to means employed.

As he emerged Into the alley, Keekie Joe, looking frightened and apprehensive, appeared out of the surrounding squalor. It was a characteristic of Keekie Joe that he always appeared without warning. A long habit of sneaking had given him this uncanny quality. Suddenly Pee-wee, in the full blush of his heroic triumph, was aware of the poor wretch shuffling along beside him.

"Wot'd they say ter yer? Wot'd yer tell 'em?" he asked fearfully.

"I didn't tell them anything," Pee-wee said. "As long as the fellers got away they won't blame you. Anyway, if you'd have been there they'd have been caught, because you didn't know those detectives because they're strangers around here."

"How'd *you* know them?" Keekie Joe inquired.

"Gee, scouts are supposed to know everything," Pee-wee informed him.

Keekie Joe gave a side glance at Pee-wee as he shuffled along at his side. He was rather interested in a class of boys who knew all officials on sight; here indeed was something worth knowing. "Yer spotted 'em?" he asked incredulously.

"*Sure* I did," said Pee-wee with great alacrity; "because scouts are supposed to be observant, see? I saw them in Northvale once. But, believe me, I didn't holla. *Oh, no!* I ran over and told the fellers and they all got away, so as long as you didn't leave them in the lurch it was all right. So now will you join the scouts? They always carry licorice jaw-breakers in their pockets," he added as a supplementary inducement; "anyway *I* do—lemon ones too, and strawberry ones."

"How many is in your gang?" Joe asked.

"Nobody yet," said Pee-wee, "because I haven't got it started. But if you'll join in with me we'll start one. You're supposed to hike and run a lot but if you want to run after fire engines and ambulances it's all right." He said this because of the favorite outdoor sport of Barrel Alley of trailing fire engines and ambulances. "So will you join?" he added.

They paused on the frontier of Joe's domain in the rear of the big bank building which fronted on Main Street. Here was the makeshift sidewalk of barrel staves whence the alley derived its name. "You have to be, kind of, you have to be a sort of a—kind of wild and reckless to join the scouts," Pee-wee pleaded. "Maybe you're kind of scared on account of thinking that you have to be civilized, but you don't; you don't even eat off plates," he added with sudden inspiration. "We cook potatoes just like tramps do, right out in the woods; we hold them on sticks over the fire. So now will you join? If you will you'll be elected patrol leader because there's only one to vote for you and I'm the one and I'm a majority. See? So if you come in right now you'll be sure to have a majority and I'll buy some Eskimo pies, too."

"Der yez swipe de pertaters?" Joe asked.

"We don't exactly kind of what you would call swipe them," Pee-wee was forced to confess. "But we get them in ways that are just as good. They taste just as good as if they were swiped, honest they do," he hastened to add. "So will you come down by the river with me? That old railroad car down there is our meeting place and it's got a stove in it and everything and there won't be any one there to-day except just you and me and we'll have an election and I'll vote for you and you can vote for yourself and so you'll be sure to be elected patrol leader. And after that I'll show you what you have to do and most of it is eating and things like that. So will you say yes?"

Keekie Joe was not to be lured by promises of "eats," though he was curious about the old railroad car. His answer to Pee-wee was characteristic of him. "I woudn' join 'em, because they're a lot of sissies," he said, "but yer needn' be ascared ter come down here because I woudn' leave no guy hurt yer; I woudn' leave 'em guy yer because yer a Boy Scout. If any of 'em starts guyen yer he'll get an upper cut, see?"

Pee-wee went on his way thoroughly disappointed and

disheartened. His thought was not that he had made a friend, but that he had lost a possible recruit. He had cherished no thought of reforming the wicked and uplifting the lowly in his effort to enlist this outlandish denizen of the slums. He was not the goody-goody little scout propagandist that we sometimes read about. He had simply been desperate and had lost all sense of discrimination. Anything would do if he could only start a patrol. What this sturdy little scout failed to understand was that in this particular enterprise the Boy Scouts had lost out but that Pee-wee Harris had won.

CHAPTER VII

APPLE BLOSSOM TIME

Pee-wee stopped in Bennett's Fresh Confectionery and regaled his drooping spirit with a chocolate soda. Then he continued his stroll up Main Street. He had always advertised his conviction that things invariably came his way but nothing came his way on this lonely Saturday morning.

He paused here and there gazing idly into shop windows, he stood gaping at a man who was having trouble with his auto, and at last he wandered into the public library. The place seemed like a tomb on that Saturday morning in the springtime. Not a boy was there to be seen. "Gee whiz, they've got something better to do than read books," he thought to himself.

There at the desk sat the librarian, silent, preoccupied. In the reading room were a few scattered readers intent on newspapers and magazines. The place, familiar and pleasant enough to Pee-wee at other times, seemed alien and uninviting at a time of day when he was usually too busy to call upon its quiet resources of treasure.

On this balmy holiday it seemed almost like school; it had

a booky, studious atmosphere which turned him against it. And to complete this impression and make the place abhorrent to him there sat Miss Bunting, the history teacher, in a corner of the reference room with several books spread about her. To Pee-wee on Saturday morning this seemed nothing less than an insult.

He approached a shelf near the librarian's desk above which was a sign that read BOOKS ESPECIALLY RECOMMENDED. Here were always a few old time favorites, worth while books made readily available. From these Pee-wee half-heartedly drew out a copy of Treasure Island and took it to a table. He knew his Treasure Island. In a disgruntled mood he sank far down in his chair and opened the book at random. He was too familiar with the enthralling pages of the famous story to seek solace in it now, but there was nothing else to do and he was too out of sorts to search further. Presently he was idly skimming over the page before him.

The appearance of the island when I came on deck next morning was altogether changed. Although the breeze had now utterly failed, we had made a great deal of way during the night, and were now lying becalmed about half a mile to the southeast of the low eastern coast. Gray-colored woods covered a large part of the surface. This even tint was indeed broken up by streaks of yellow sandbreak in the lower lands, and by many tall trees of the pine family, out-topping the others—some singly, some in clumps; but the general coloring was uniform and sad. The hills ran up...

Pee-wee blinked his eyes, yawned, then suddenly drew himself up into an erect sitting posture and pushed the book from him. "Gee whiz," he mused, "that's what I'd like, to go off to a desert island. They don't have any desert islands now; that's one thing I don't like about this century. Hikes and camping and all that make me tired; I'd like to be on a desert island, that's what *I'd* like to do. I'd like to be marooned. Gee whiz, we only kid ourselves trying to make ourselves think we're doing things that are wild. I guess all the desert islands are discovered by now; oh boy, there were lots and lots of them in the seventeenth century; that's my favorite century, the seventeenth, on account of buried treasure and desert islands."

Indulging these disconsolate spring musings, Pee-wee sank down in his chair again, a frowning, dreamy figure, and floated out of the library and away from all the sordid environments of Bridgeboro toward a desert island situated in the south-eastern part of the seventeenth century. It was a long, long way off and he had to cross the eighteenth and nineteenth centuries to get to it. He was no longer a pioneer scout now, nor a scout at all, but a doughty explorer about to set foot for the first time on soil that white man had never trod before.

He sank farther down in his chair as he voyaged afar. He was soon out of sight of land and almost out of sight of the few readers in that drowsy old library. He continued to sink lower and lower in his chair as if he had sprung a leak. Only his round, curly head was above the table. The island which he reached was a delectable spot, an earthly Paradise, with trees laden with fruit which came down like summer showers when he shook the trees. He wandered about on the enchanted shores, and ate so much fruit that oddly he felt that he was himself a tree and that some one was trying to shake fruit out of him.... He sat up with a start and found himself confronting the smiling countenance of Miss Warden, the librarian, who had been shaking him not unkindly.

"Where have you been?" she asked, laughing.

"To a desert island," said Pee-wee.

He roused himself and wandered out into the balmy air and down toward the river, a lonesome little figure. A broad field bordered the stream and crossing this he approached the old car which was the troops' head-quarters. But before he reached it he was aware of something which caused him to rub his eyes and stare. As sure as he lived, there in front of him was the seventeenth century, F. O. B. Bridgeboro, with all appurtenances and accessories. He stood gaping at a little island out in the middle of the stream, which had no more business there than Pee-wee had had to be dozing in the library.

Pee-wee stood stark still in the middle of the field and rubbed his eyes to make sure that he was awake. There was not the slightest doubt that what he saw was very real. The river at that point was quite wide and its opposite shore was bordered with sparse woodland.

Pee-wee had bathed and fished and canoed in this neighborhood almost as long as he could remember and he was perfectly certain that there had never been an island there. He knew an island when he saw one and nothing was more certain than that this one was a stranger in the neighborhood.

Yet it seemed to be perfectly at home out there in the middle of the stream, just as if it had been born there and had grown up there. There was nothing fugitive looking about it at all. In the true spirit of the twentieth century, which is all for time saving and convenience, it had voyaged to Pee-wee, thereby saving him the time and perils of an extended cruise. It had, as one might say, been delivered at his door.

This was certainly an improvement over the old, out-of-date method of desert island exploration. Such patent, adjustable islands would bring the joys of adventurous pioneering "within the reach of all" as advertisement writers are so fond of declaring, just as the phonograph, has brought music into every home.

"That's funny," said Pee-wee, pausing in amazement. "That wasn't here yesterday, because I was down here yesterday. Anyway as long as no one's here I'm going to be the one to go and discover it. Findings is keepings; it's just the same with islands as it is with everything else."

To increase his astonishment and cause his brimming cup of joy to overflow a tree stood upon the little speck of green land laden with white blossoms, which wafted a faint but fragrant promise to the enchanted scout upon the distant shore.

"That's an apple tree," said Pee-wee, his mouth watering. "I'm going over there to discover it and then it's mine, the whole island's mine because findings is keepings, that's international law."

No doubt he felt that the League of Nations would stand in back of him in the matter of this epoch-making discovery.

Percy Keese Fitzhugh

CHAPTER VIII

PEE-WEE EXPLORES THE ISLAND

There was no doubt at all of the reality of this extra-ordinary apparition. Pee-wee, who was always sure of everything, was doubly sure of this. Squint and rub his eyes as he would, there was the desert island in the middle of the river with the tree surmounting it. By all the precedents in history this island was his. He had as much right to it as the king of Spain had to San Salvador, more in fact, for the king of Spain had never seen the island of San Salvador.

If there was any good in history at all (and Pee-wee had his doubts about that) why then this mysterious island belonged to him. Miss Bunting, if she had any sense of fairness at all, would concede this. If the good old rule of findings is keepings applied to monarchs it certainly applied to Boy Scouts. So Pee-wee prepared to set sail and formally take possession of his discovery. He would sail around it as Columbus had sailed around the coast of Cuba....

Entering the troops' deserted old car he got the oars of the old flat bottom boat belonging to the troop. He also procured a black marking stick used for marking scout signs on rocks, and a pasteboard target on the back of which he printed in ostentatious lettering.

THIS DESERT ISLAND IS DISCOVERED
BY WALTER HARRIS AND ALL PRETAINING
TO IT INCLUDING APPLES AND
EVERYTHING AND OTHER KINDS OF
FOOD AND WILD ANIMALS IF THERE
ARE ANY ALSO PRESIOUS METTLES AND
ALL NATIVES MUST SWEAR TO WALTER
HARRIS I MEAN THEY MUST SWEAR
ALLEAGANCE AND SAID WALTER
HARRIS SHALL HAVE THE RIGHT OF
SETTLEMENT.

P. S. ESPECIALLY APPLES.

Having thus established his rights according to the most historical rule for the acquisition of new territory, Pee-wee set sail in his gallant bark and after an uneventful voyage of seven minutes drew his boat half-way up the rugged shore.

Though his back was toward the island during the entire cruise, he knew that land was near fully a minute and a half before reaching it by the presence of several grass-hoppers kicking vainly in the surf. But what particularly attracted his attention as indicating the presence of human life upon the island was part of a cruller bobbing near the shore. This startled and impressed him as the footprint in the sand startled and impressed Robinson Crusoe.

Pee-wee could hardly believe that on the very day which had begun so inauspiciously he had actually set foot upon a strange island, but there it was under his very feet and it could not get away for he was standing on it.

Percy Keese Fitzhugh

Having fastened his sign to the tree trunk he proceeded to explore the island. This was done mainly with his eyes since the island was too small for the usual form of exploration.

It consisted of a little spot of land about fifteen feet in diameter, held together by the roots of the tree. It was hubbly and grass-covered and one side of it had a kind of ragged edge. It seemed to be subject to earthquakes for as Pee-wee stood upon it he felt a slight jarring beneath him. Undoubtedly the island depended on the tree more than the tree depended on the island; one might have fancied that the island carried too much soil.

But Pee-wee's surprise at the instability of his Conquest was nothing to his astonishment at the voice which he presently heard above him.

"Hello, what are you doing down there?"

Pee-wee looked up and beheld a boy seated comfortably in the branches of the tree. He was looking down through the profusion of blossoms with an exceedingly merry face, and had apparently been witnessing the arrival of the discoverer with silent amusement.

"Some desert island, hey?" he laughed.

"Are you a native?" Pee-wee shouted.

"Sure, I'm part of the wild life of the island, I'm a scout," the boy called down. "Come on up, there's room for two on this branch. If the island should lurch you might get your feet wet."

"What is this island anyway?" Pee-wee asked, somewhat

taken aback by the discovery that he was not the discoverer. "Where does it belong? Anyway I'm the boss of it because I discovered it. I just put my sign up and you can come down and see it if you want to and swear allegiance."

"What are you talking about?" the boy called down. "I was on it before it was born."

"Do you mean to tell me I didn't discover you?" Pee-wee shouted up.

"No, *I* discovered *you*," said the other boy.

"What do you mean, *you knew it before it was born*?" Pee-wee demanded skeptically. "How could it have been before it was? If a thing isn't, how can you know it? You're crazy. I was the first one to discover it since it was here and you're a part of it. But anyway I'd like to know how it got here, that's one thing *I'd* like to know."

"Come on up here and I'll tell you," said the wild native.

Pee-wee climbed up and sat on the limb beside his new friend. He was a boy somewhat older than Pee-wee with a face so round that the face of the man in the moon would have seemed narrow by comparison. And there was a redness in his cheeks which made his head seem almost like an apple grown prematurely ripe upon that blossom laden tree. He wore the negligee scout attire and his happy-go-lucky nature was made the more piquant by the easy, humorous fashion in which he sat upon the limb, swinging his legs.

Pee-wee could not have found it in his heart to quarrel with any boy whose face looked so much like an apple, and, moreover, it was apparent that here was a boy whom it would be utterly impossible to quarrel with on any ground whatever—or in any tree whatever.

"Gee whiz, this is a funny thing," Pee-wee said; "I was kind of making believe that I was an explorer, but anyway I'm glad you're here."

"I'm here because I'm here," said the other boy.

"Gee, I can't deny that," said Pee-wee.

"It doesn't make any difference to me," said the boy; "I'd just as soon be in one place as another."

"As long as it's not school," said Pee-wee.

"Oh, that's understood," said the other boy; "let's talk of something pleasant."

"I bet there'll be a lot of apples here later," said Pee-wee; "when it's vacation, hey?"

"I don't know whether they'll be here," said the other boy, "because you can't trust this blamed island over night, but they'll be on the tree, wherever it is, and the way to find them will be to look for the tree."

"*You said it*," said Pee-wee. "What's your name?"

"Roland Poland," said the boy; "Roly Poly for short."

"Mine's Walter Harris, but they call me Pee-wee. How did this island get here anyway?"

"It started being an island under my very feet," said Roly

Poly. "There are five scouts in my patrol besides myself; we're just getting started—"

"I'm the only one in my patrol," Pee-wee interrupted. "Where do you come from?"

"From North Bridgeboro," said Roly Poly, swinging his legs. "The six of us went to camp for the day just above old Trimmer's land up the river."

"I know him," Pee-wee said; "he's a grouch."

"Very muchly," said Roly; "he's worse than algebra."

"He's worse than algebra and civil government put together," said Pee-wee.

"Did you say *civil*?" said Roly Poly; "don't mention civil in the same sentence with him; he's the man that put the crab in crab-apple."

"He's got a dandy orchard, though," said Pee-wee.

"Sure, this is a part of it," said Roly Poly.

CHAPTER IX

THE LOOKOUT SEES A SAIL

"*Good night,*" said Pee-wee; "I don't blame it for going away from him. Can he take it back? It's an island now and it's part of Bridgeboro. He can't take it on account of international law; that's what *I* think. How did it happen?"

"It's a very short story," said his new friend; "it's only about a mile and a half long—from North Bridgeboro down to here. We were camping in Wallace's grove and a little way down the river we saw a kind of a little spot of land with a tree on it. There were lots of apple trees all around there near the shore. We didn't know that orchard belonged to old Trimmer."

"He thinks he owns the whole river," said Pee-wee.

"That little spot of land stuck out sort of like a balcony on account of it being near the bend of the river; the river coming around the bend sort of scooped a place out underneath it; it was all under-mined—"

"I know what happened! I know what happened!" Pee-wee shouted. "I know the place, it was nice and shady underneath it and you could go under it in a canoe; lots of times I did."

"Well, you never will any more," said Roly Poly.

"Go on, tell me! Go on, tell me!" Pee-wee encouraged excitedly.

"There was a pole sticking out of the water right near there," Pee-wee's new friend continued, "and we thought it meant there was good fishing there. So I said I'd go and see if I could catch a couple of eels and sunfish or something. While I was out at the edge of that little knob of land or whatever you want to call it, all of a sudden I could feel something giving way under me and the first thing I knew the whole business was in the water.

"Oh, you should have heard those fellows laugh as I went sailing down the river. That was about ten o'clock this morning and the tide was running down strong. This little old island flopped around and went every which way but it stayed right side up anyway and do you think I'd desert the ship? By the time we flopped downstream this far the tide was so low that our little old roots dragged the bottom and we stopped for keeps. So here we are till the tide comes in anyway. I don't know whether we'll float in deep water or not, or whether we'll capsize in deep water or not and I don't know anything about international law, but a life on the ocean wave for *me*."

"I know all about international law," Pee-wee shouted. "Real estate is in a certain place, isn't it? If a man owns real estate it's bounded by something, isn't it? Well, then, if it isn't bounded by those things any more how can it belong to that same man? If a man owns land in a certain place and it stops being in that place, whose is it?"

Percy Keese Fitzhugh

"Search me," said Roly Poly.

"Besides I've got an inspiration; do you know what those are?" Pee-wee vociferated.

"Have you got it with you?"

"*Sure* I've got it with me! Don't I always have them with me?"

Roly Poly seemed amused.

"There are two kinds of scouts, aren't there?" Pee-wee asked vociferously. "Regular scouts and sea scouts. Sea scouts are supposed to live on the water and regular scouts are supposed to live under the trees, like. So we can do both and we'll be combination scouts. We'll be the Combination Scouts of America, hey? Will you?"

"I'll be anything as long as it's Saturday; I'm not particular," said Roly Poly.

"Because my father knows a man that's a lawyer and he'll stick up for us," Pee-wee continued excitedly. "Because old Trimmer hasn't got any deed that says he owns an island, has he? All right, this is an island in Bridgeboro. You can't deny that, can you? Let's hear you deny that. All right, then, if he comes and tries to get this island, he'll be trespassing, won't he? And so we'll start the Combination Scouts of America and we'll call ourselves the—the—the—"

"The Sardine Patrol," suggested Roly.

"We'll call ourselves the Crab-apple Patrol," said Pee-wee, "because apples are on land and crabs are in the water. Will you?"

"I see a sail on the horizon," said Roly.

"If it's old Trimmer let me handle him," said Pee-wee.

"It's the rest of the patrol," said Roly. "Do you see those two canoes coming around the bend? We'll have a meeting of the general staff and decide what to do."

"Whatever we do, we'll do something, hey?" said Pee-wee.

"More than that," said Roly.

"Anyway, we'll start a patrol or something, hey?"

"Oh, we'll start something, leave it to us," said Roly Poly.

CHAPTER X

THE OTHERS ARRIVE

The arrival of the five North Bridgeboro scouts was the occasion of much merriment and banter. These boys from the small village up the river had formed themselves into a patrol but they were two members short of the required number and they had no scoutmaster.

Whether they took scouting seriously it would be hard to say; if so it must have been a great comfort to them to have wished upon their budding organization such an instructor and propagandist as the diminutive genius whom they were now about to meet. Whatever material they had among them for progress in the scouting field, they gave every indication of possessing that quality of unholy mirth which distinguished the notorious Silver Foxes. Perhaps their silver was not quite so bright, but they gave promise.

"Hey, where are you going with the apple tree?" one of them called from the nearest canoe. "What are you trying to do? Swipe a chunk of property? That's a part of North Bridgeboro you've got there."

"Why didn't you take the whole village?" another called.

"Hey, Roly, where are you going with the real estate?" another called.

"I knew you were too heavy for that neck of land," shouted another.

"Why didn't you take the whole orchard with you?" a third wanted to know.

"*For the love of—*," another ejaculated. "Look at the sign, will you! The place is discovered already!"

Pee-wee did not wait for formal introductions. "We're going to start the Combination Scouts of Bridgeboro!" he shouted. "We're going to be sea scouts and land scouts all rolled into one! We took possession and it's all right! Old Trimmer can't say that he owned an island, can he? We're going to have our pictures in *Boys' Life* and everything and we're going to have all the apples when they're ripe and maybe we're going to call ourselves the Crab-apple Patrol! Maybe there's treasure buried here, how do we know? And we're going to get one of those things—a saxophone or whatever you call it—to take our latitude and longitude with! We're going to be better than the Ravens and the Elks and the Silver Foxes and I know how to make apple-sauce! We're going to be a new kind of a patrol!"

"In the name of goodness, what's that, a phonograph?" one of the approaching canoeists called.

"That's the discoverer," Roly called back. "He took possession of the island in the name of the King of Bridgeboro."

"I thought it was an earthquake," laughed a tall boy who

was stepping ashore.

"Oh, we have those too," laughed Roly; "all the latest improvements. That's Pee-wee; he's perfectly harmless, step right ashore, you're all welcome."

"You're stepping into the seventeenth century," Pee-wee shouted, descending precipitately out of the tree.

"The seventeenth century must have been very wet," said the tall boy as he lifted one foot out of the water only to plunge the other into the ragged, muddy edge of the island, in his efforts to get on shore. It was very funny to see him wallow In the water, seeking foothold on the submerged tentacles of root, ever slipping, and always with the soberest look on his face. "This must be the back entrance," he said. "Where are we supposed to park?"

This tall boy, who turned out to be a sort of patrol leader and scoutmaster in one, had a kind of whimsical look of inquiry on his face which was his permanent expression, and which was made the more humorous by red hair which he wore decidedly pompadour. There was that in his look which indicated his taking everything as he found it, his attitude being always quietly humorous and never surprised.

His demeanor, in whatever adventure befell, seemed always that of an amiable victim placing himself at the mercy of his enterprising comrades and going through every kind of outlandish escapade and adventure with a ludicrously sober look on his funny face. To him everything that happened seemed part of the game of life and he appeared never in the least astonished at anything.

To see him soberly going through with some adventure

which the sprightly genius of his associates had conceived was as good as a circus. Naturally such a fellow was called "old" and they called him Old Rip and Good Old Rip and Doctor Rip and Professor Rip. His name was Townsend Ripley.

Townsend began at the very beginning to take the irrepressible ex-Raven very soberly indeed, and the more preposterous Pee-wee's schemes the more in favor of them Townsend seemed to be. No doubt he got a great deal of amusement out of Pee-wee. But Pee-wee never knew it.

CHAPTER XI

PLANS

It was quite characteristic of Townsend Ripley that he did not ask Roly Poly anything about his extraordinary adventure. Amid the chorus of exclamations and inquiries he preserved a quiet, whimsical demeanor, glancing about as if rather interested in this desert island. There it was, and that was enough for him.

"If this island is going to keep moving you'll have to put a license plate on it, Roly," he drawled. "First thing you know you'll have the inland waterway inspectors after you. You're blocking up the channel too. Why didn't you drift down as far as Southbridge where the taxes aren't so high?"

"I was—I was thinking about it," Pee-wee suddenly burst forth like a cyclone, "and there are a lot of things we can do—I've got a lot of ideas—there are seven things and we can do any one of them!"

"Why not do them all?" Ripley asked.

"That's just what *I* say," Pee-wee shouted.

"Or we can each do a different thing," Ripley suggested. "There are just seven of us. Anything suits me."

"Do you want to know how I discovered it?" Pee-wee said excitedly.

"No, as long as we know it's discovered, that's enough," said Ripley.

"I discovered it, then he discovered me," said Pee-wee, "but I'm the discoverer because it wasn't an island when he got on it, see. Anyway, that man can't take it, can he? So will you start a patent combination patrol? And I vote for you to be the leader!"

"Let's see if we can't start the island," suggested Ripley.

"We don't want to start a Bridgeboro patrol and then find that we're in Southbridge!" said one of the boys whom the others called Nuts.

"Oh, I don't see why not," drawled Townsend; "trouble is," he added, glancing casually about, "we can't go on any hikes. If we start skirting the coast we'll get dizzy."

"I know what we can do," said Pee-wee, "because, gee whiz, we've got to have exercise, that's one sure thing. If we can make the island go round why then we can keep walking like a—like a—you know—like a horse on a treadmill—hey? And we won't get dizzy at all, because it'll be the island that goes round, see?"

"That's a very good suggestion," said Townsend, "but suppose on one of our long hikes we want to stop and camp. As soon as we stop hiking we'll start going round backward with the island."

"We should worry," said Pee-wee.

"Oh, we're not going to worry," said Townsend.

"You said it," vociferated Pee-wee. "Do you know why I like you? Because you're—you know—you're kind of—sort of—"

"Absolutely," said Townsend. "You read me like a book."

"This is better than books," said Pee-wee, "because this is a kind of a desert island and a ship, isn't it? So will you all stay here till I get back, because I'm going to get my tent and some eats and a lot of stuff for camping and then we'll start our patrol."

"I can't say that we'll stay here," said Townsend, "but we'll stick to the island. I have a hunch that this island is going to put one over on us. If we're not here when you get back you'd better advertise in the 'Lost and Found' column of the Bridgeboro paper, 'Lost, one desert island. Finder will be suitably rewarded upon returning same to the patent adjustable scouts—'"

"Not adjustable—*combination*," Pee-wee corrected. "Do you like roasted potatoes? I know how to roast them. And I'll get some bacon, too; shall I?"

"Suppose you should be captured by your parents while you're on the mainland," Townsend inquired.

"Then I'll send you a smoke signal," Pee-wee said, "and you can come and talk to my mother, because she'll be sure to listen to you because, anyway, you've got a lot of sense."

"And several of us will canoe up to North Bridgeboro and get some stuff and tell our folks and we'll be back in an hour because the tide's starting to run up," said a boy they called Billy.

"If you have any trouble with the folks just give me a smoke signal and I'll canoe up," drawled Townsend.

"Good old Rip," chorused half a dozen voices.

The boy they called Billy turned to Pee-wee and whispered, "Don't worry about your folks. Old Rip makes a specialty of parents; they all eat out of his hands, fathers especially. As soon as they see him they surrender."

"I make a specialty of cooks," Pee-wee said. "Our cook gives me everything I want. And anyway we couldn't starve because scouts can't starve; they can eat roots and herbs and things; I'll show you. Do you like chocolate marshmallows? Even scouts can eat moss to keep from starving. And they can't get lost either—I'll show you how."

Pee-wee decided to take one of the boys with him to prove to his mother that the island was inhabited, and two other boys started back up the river in the other canoe. This left Townsend with two companions on the island. He sat against the trunk of the tree, knees drawn up, philosophically scanning the shore and occasionally giving an expectant glance up the river for smoke signals. He seemed resigned to a quiet expectancy that he would be summoned to intercede in one quarter or another. He looked very whimsical and funny.

"I wonder if you have to crank this island or whether it has a self-starter," he drawled in his amusing way. "If they don't get back by one or so, we'll have to make some root sandwiches. What do you say, Charlie!"

CHAPTER XII

THE DISCOVERER RETURNS

In about an hour and a half the two boys from up the river returned with provisions.

"Any news from the discoverer?" they asked.

"I think he's being held as a hostage by the cook," said Townsend. "Shall we land and lay waste to his home?"

"Oh, I think we can safely leave everything to him," said Billy. "What do you think of the discoverer, anyway?"

"I'm for the discoverer first, last and always," said Townsend. "He has only to lead and I'll follow. Now that we've met him I feel that life without the discoverer would not be worth living. I'm glad that next week is Easter vacation, because we couldn't think of school and the discoverer at the same time. He's more than a scout, he's an institution.

"Do you know, Charlie, I think we're moving? We were almost opposite that old railroad car a few minutes ago. Either Bridgeboro is going down or we're going up. Do you feel the climate changing? You don't suppose this

Percy Keese Fitzhugh

island is going to go up the river again and join old Trimmer's orchard, do you?"

"Maybe it's homesick," said a boy they called Brownie.

"I hope the discoverer will discover it," said Billy.

"We'd better scatter something in our trail," said Townsend soberly, "so that he can follow. I think that's the regulation thing for scouts to do, isn't it?"

He had been whittling a stick and now with a sober look he began throwing the chips into the water as if to indicate the path of the departing island. "That's what you call blazing a trail," he said; "if he's a scout he can follow."

The little island was now moving slowly upstream by the incoming tide. It caught on the flats, performed a slow pirouette like some drowsy toe-dancer or exhausted merry-go-round, then extricated itself and floated majestically in the channel till the little apple tree became involved with the foliage along shore.

"Do you know this seems like a very funny kind of an island to me?" Townsend Ripley drawled. "I wonder what makes it hold together? It ought to disintegrate."

"Dis what?" asked Billy.

"Disintegrate—that's Latin for falling to pieces."

"Maybe the roots hold it together," said Roland.

"It ought to dissolve," said Townsend. "This land doesn't seem to be soluble in water. The coast all around ought to wash away. There is something mysterious here. This island is as solid as a pancake; I don't understand it. By all the rules of the game there shouldn't be anything left here but the tree by this evening. There doesn't seem to be any process of erosion."

"What will we do If the island washes away from under us?" asked the boy they called Brownie. "The tree'll fall over sideways, won't it? I don't want to camp on an island that keeps getting smaller all the time. It's bad enough to have a tent shrink after a rain, but *an island*!"

"I think this island is warranted not to shrink," said Townsend.

"Warranted nothing," said Billy; "look how muddy the water is all around it. It'll be about as big as a fifty cent piece by midnight. The river is eating it all away."

"Speaking of eating," said Townsend, "here comes the discoverer."

The discoverer and his companion were indeed approaching and apparently they had sacked the town of Bridgeboro. Their gallant barque labored under a veritable mountain of miscellaneous paraphernalia and out of the pile projected a long bar with a device on the end of it which glinted red and green in the sunshine.

"It looks like a weather-vane," said Billy.

"There's something printed on it," said Roly.

"It says *STOP*," said the boy they called Nuts.

"It says *GO*" said the boy they called Brownie.

"I think," said Townsend, scrutinizing the approaching transport in his funny way, "I think, I *think*, it's a traffic sign. You don't see any automobiles in the canoe, do you?"

"There's something sticking out on the left side," said Billy; "I think it's a Ford. I hope the island isn't going to be overrun by motorists."

"It's not a Ford, it's a dishpan," said Brownie.

"They're the same thing," said Townsend. "What is that on the duffel bag—a license plate?"

Suddenly the voice of the discoverer floated across the expanse of sun-flickered water. "We're going to have hunter's stew for supper and I'm going to make it and my mother says I can stay all through Easter vacation and I got a lot of things out of our attic. Do you like bananas? I've got a whole bunch and I've got a lot of new ideas— dandy ones! I know how to fry them! I know how to slice them and fry them!"

"I'd like to try some fried ideas," said Townsend. "I don't think I ever ate them sliced before."

It may be said that Pee-wee's ideas, whether fried or baked or boiled or roasted, were usually underdone and required to be put back into the oven.

Be that as it may, he soon proceeded to unload these, as well as the interesting junk which he had gathered, the most surprising object of which was the dilapidated revolving traffic sign lately discarded by the Bridgeboro police department in favor of a lighthouse or silent cop, so called.

This acquisition was the pride of Pee-wee's life; its heavy metal stand had long since gone the way of all junk and it could not stand unsupported. As Pee-wee plunged it heroically in the earth and stood holding it with one hand he looked not unlike Columbus planting the flaunting emblem of Ferdinand and Isabella on the shore of San Salvador, except that this tableau of the well known historical episode was somewhat marred by the fact of his holding a half eaten banana in his other hand. But his new friends stared with all the amazement shown by the natives upon the landing of that other great discoverer. Only a specific inventory can do justice to the provisions and furniture which Pee-wee brought.

One revolving police traffic sign
One large phonograph horn
One dishpan full of crullers (taken in a masterly assault upon the Harris pantry)
One tent
One duffel bag with cooking set
Part of a vacuum cleaner
One scout belt axe
One Thanksgiving horn
One automobile siren horn.
One lantern
Two long clothesline supporters
A towel-rack that opened like a fan
A skein of clothesline
A small kitchen-range shovel
Two boxes filled with canned goods
One box filled with loose edibles
One ice cream freezer

"Didn't you bring a cow?" Townsend asked. "We can never make ice cream without cream."

"We're in reach of the mainland, aren't we?" Pee-wee retorted thunderously. "It isn't as if we were going out of sight of land; gee whiz, then I'd have brought quite a lot of stuff."

"Oh, I see," said Townsend.

"I just picked up a few odds and ends," Pee-wee explained. "I'm going to make a couple of more trips tomorrow."

"If you happen to think of it bring a lawnmower," said Townsend; "they come in handy. And a few life preservers if you happen to have any, in case the island goes to pieces."

"How can it go to pieces?" Pee-wee demanded. "Islands don't go to pieces, do they? Australia is an island, isn't it? It's just where it always was, isn't it? You're crazy! All we need is one more scout and I know one by the name of Keekie Joe, and I'm going to try to get him and then we'll be a full patrol and I decided to name it the Alligators, because they belong on land and water both and we're sea scouts on the land kind of, so maybe I'll decide to name it the Turtles, maybe."

"Discoverer," said Townsend, "we're with you whatever you do, but there is a mystery about this island which I would like to fathom before we organize—"

"I fathomed lots of mysteries," shouted Pee-wee.

"I don't know whether you know what erosion means—"

"Sure I know what it means," said Pee-wee; "it means getting rusty, kind of."

"It means land being washed away by water. If you put a piece of land in the water, the water will dissolve it and it won't take long either. It isn't like an island that has always been where it is—a kind of hill sticking up out of the water. This is just a piece of land and the roots of this little tree won't hold it together long.

"The question is, should we go hunting for new members under those conditions? Pretty soon we'll have a full patrol and no island under us; we'll be in the water. That's perfectly agreeable to me and all the rest of us. But does Keekie Joe know how to swim? We really have no *grounds* for forming a patrol. See?"

"Do you call that an argument?" Pee-wee thundered. "It shows how much you know about geography because look at an ice cream soda! Does that corrode? Let's hear you answer that? Or erode or whatever you call it. A chunk of ice cream floats in the soda, doesn't it? Maybe after a while it melts, but this land isn't ice cream, is it?

"That shows how much you know about logic. This island has been here ever since early this morning, hasn't it? And it's just as big as it was, isn't it? An island is an island and the water won't melt it unless it's hot—like a lump of sugar in a cup of coffee. You've got to stir it up to melt it. Is North America corroding? Or Coney Island? Is this island any smaller than it was?"

"No, it isn't, and that's the funny part," said Townsend. "We've explored the coast but we haven't explored the depths. Let's have that little shovel a minute, will you?"

CHAPTER XIII

"STOP"

The ice cream soda argument was not a good one at all, for no lump of ice cream ever remained long intact where Pee-wee was. Whether it melted or not, it disappeared. And why this freakish little island did not rapidly dissolve was a mystery.

By all the laws it should have melted away, leaving the deserted tree to topple over and form a new obstruction to boating. But there it was floating more easily as the tide rose, with apparently no intention of allowing itself to be absorbed by the surrounding waters. It is true that a belt of muddy water bordered its wild and forbidding coast and that its shore line was of a consistency suitable for the making of mud pies, but its body seemed as solid and resistant as a rock.

Pee-wee always claimed that it was he and he alone who discovered the mysterious secret of Merry-go-round Island; he and he alone who penetrated its unknown depths. In this bold exploration a courageous sardine sandwich played an important part and out of sheer gratitude Pee-wee, from that time forward, was ever partial to sardine sandwiches, regarding them with tender and grateful affection.

He was standing near the apple tree holding the traffic sign like a pilgrim's banner beside him and, as has been told, eating a banana with the other hand. That fact is well established. Little he thought that when Roly Poly, delving into a paper bag that was in a grocery box, handed him a sardine sandwich, it would mark an epoch in scout history.

In order to accept the proffered refreshment, Pee-wee was compelled either to relinquish the traffic sign or the banana. One moment of frantic consideration held him, then in a burst of inspiration he plunged the metal standard deep into the ground, and took the sardine sandwich in his free hand. The printed cross-piece on the traffic sign joggled around so that just as he plunged his mouth into the sandwich the word GO made an appropriate announcement to his comrades. It is hard to say what might have happened if Townsend Ripley had not turned the sign so that it said STOP just as Pee-wee consumed the last mouthful.

"Isstrucsmlikewood," ejaculated Pee-wee, consuming the last mouthful. "Issoundlkbo—boards!"

Billy was quick to raise the bar of the traffic sign and plunge it down again. It was certainly no tentacle of root that the probing bar struck, but something hard, yet ever so slightly yielding, something which gave forth a hollow sound.

It was easy to explore America after Columbus had shown the way and it was a simple matter now for Townsend, with the little shovel, to dig a hole three or four feet deep about the traffic sign. The boys all kneeled about, peering in as if buried treasure were there, until an area of muddy wood was revealed. Roly Poly knocked it with a rock and the noise convinced them that the wood was of considerable area and that probably *nothing was beneath it.*

"Well—what—do—you—know—about—that?" Billy asked incredulously.

"Jab it down somewhere else," said Brownie.

Pee-wee moved the metal rod a yard or so distant and plunged it in the ground again. There was the same hollow sound. For a moment they all sat spellbound, mystified. Then, as if seized by a sudden thought, Brownie hurried to the edge of the little island, exploring with his hands. He lifted up some grassy soil that drooped and hung in the water, and tore it away. As he did so there was revealed a ridge of heavy wood over which it had hung. By the same process he exposed a yard or two of this black mud-covered edge.

"Well—I'll—be—*jiggered!*" said Billy.

"It's a scow or something!" said Brownie, almost too astonished to speak.

"The island seems to overlap it sort of like a pie-crust," drawled Townsend.

"The scow is the undercrust!" shouted Pee-wee, delighted with this comparison to his favorite edible. "We'll call it Apple-pie Island and it can't corrode or erode or whatever you call it, either, because it's boxed in!"

That indeed seemed to be the way of it. Apparently the

island reposed comfortably in and over the edges of a huge, shallow box of heavy timbers which had received it with kindly hospitality when it broke away and toppled over into the water. As we know, the river had eaten away the land under the little balcony peninsula, and the scow, or whatever it was, must have drifted or been moored underneath the earthy projection.

"Maybe it belonged to that big dredge that was working up here," said Pee-wee, "Anyway it's lucky for us, hey? Because now our island has a good foundation and it can't dis—what d'you call it."

"Only it complicates the question of ownership," said Townsend, apparently not in the least astonished or excited. "Here is a piece of land belonging to old Trimmer on a scow or something or other belonging to a dredging company or somebody or other and claimed by the boy scouts by right of discovery."

"Old Trimmer owned the land," Pee-wee fairly yelled, "but now the land isn't there any more and now it's an island so he doesn't own it because he's got a deed and it doesn't say *island* on the deed! *Gee whiz*, anybody knows that."

"But suppose the owner of the scow wants his property," Townsend said.

"Let him come and get it," Pee-wee shouted. "If we get a deed for this island the scow is covered by the deed!"

"You mean it's covered by the island," Brownie said.

"Well, we seem to be standing still now, anyway," said Townsend; "it's a relief to know that when we wake up to-morrow morning we won't be floating in the water. Who's got a match? Let's start a fire and begin moving toward the hunter's stew."

"We don't need matches," Pee-wee said with a condescending sneer. "Do you think scouts use matches? They light fires by rubbing sticks. Matches are civilized."

Whereupon Pee-wee gave a demonstration of not getting a light by the approved old Indian fashion of rubbing sticks and striking sparks from stones and so on.

"Here comes a man down the river in a motorboat," said Nuts; "turn the stop sign that way and we'll ask him for a match."

Pee-wee, somewhat subdued by his failure, confronted the approaching boat with the red panel which said STOP, and held his hand up like a traffic officer.

But there was no need of requiring the approaching voyager to pause. For he had every intention of pausing. Neither would there have been any use of asking him for a match. For he never gave away matches.

Old Trimmer never gave away anything. He would not even give away a secret, he was so stingy. To get a match from old Trimmer you would have had to give him chloroform. It was said that he would not look at his watch to see what time it was for fear of wearing it out, and that he looked over the top of his spectacles to save the lenses. At all events he was so economical that he seldom wasted any words, and the words that he did waste were not worth saving; they were not very nice words.

CHAPTER XIV

"GO"

Old Trimmer chugged up to the edge of the island in the shabbiest, leakiest little motor dory on the river, and grasped a little tuft of greensward to keep his boat from drifting.

"Well, now, what's all this?" he began. "What you youngsters been doin' up the river, eh?"

"This used to be your land before it was an island," said Pee-wee diplomatically. "I bet you'll say it's funny how it used to be your apple tree and everything. But it broke away and kind of fell down and now it's an island and we discovered it. It can't—one thing—it can't ever be a peninsula again, that's sure. Islands, they're discovered and then you own them, that's the way it is. Findings is keepings with islands."

"Is that so?" said old Trimmer, half-interested and examining what might be called the underpinning of the island with keen preoccupation.

"Well, you'll just clear off'n this here property double quick. Pile in here and I'll set you ashore."

"Don't you go," urged Pee-wee; "we've got a right here; we're going to camp on this island."

"Sure we are," said Roly Poly.

"And you can't make us get off, either, because it isn't on your land."

Old Trimmer wasted no words. "Pile in here, all of you," he said, indicating the boat, "or I'll have yer all up fer trespassin'."

"Do you own this old scow or whatever it is underneath us?" Townsend asked quietly.

"Look a'here, young feller, no talkin' back," said old Trimmer testily; "come along, step lively. I'm going to tow this whole business back up to where it belongs. Now d'ye want me ter set yer ashore or not?"

"Not," said Roly Poly.

"I don't think we have anything to say about it, Mr. Trimmer," said Townsend. "The land that used to be part of your field seems to be on a scow or something or other and we're on the land that's on the scow. We're here because we're here—"

"Let's hear you answer that argument!" shouted Pee-wee in a voice of thunder. "This is a river, isn't it? Do you deny that? It's an inward waterway—I mean inland—and it belongs to the government and this scow or whatever it is, is on it and something that used to be a peninsula but isn't any more is on the scow and we're on the thing that used to be a peninsula—"

"In the shade of the young apple tree," said Townsend.

"That's just what I was going to say," said Pee-wee, "and you can't put us off this land because if that's trespassing then the land is trespassing too—it's trespassing on the scow—so we won't get off the land till you take the land off the scow and put it back where it belongs and then we'll get off it because, gee whiz, scouts have no right to trespass." He paused, not for lack of arguments but for lack of breath.

"So that's the way it is, is it?" said old Trimmer darkly. "Well, we'll see."

"Sure we'll see," said Pee-wee. "That shows how much you know about geography and international law and all those things. Suppose Cape Cod should break off and float away. Would it belong to New Hampshire any more—I mean Connecticut—I mean Massachusetts? Gee whiz, we're going to stay right here because we're on a public waterway and anyway you don't own the scow that this land is on, do you?"

There was, of course, no answer to this fine analysis of the legal points involved.

"That there scow was under my land," said old Trimmer.

"It was in the river and it wasn't on anybody's land as I understand it," said Townsend in his funny way. "Your land trespassed on the scow—"

"Sure it did!" interrupted Pee-wee. "It really had no right to do that, Mr. Trimmer, unless you can show that you own the scow. As I understand it this is a kind of a legal sandwich. The land that used to be a part of your field is between the scow and us—"

"Sure it is!" vociferated Pee-wee, caught by the idea of a sandwich so huge and picturesque. "We're kind of like one of the slices of breads and the scow is the other slice. It's thick and dark like rye bread," he added to make the picture more graphic.

"It's a kind of a legal sandwich," said Townsend, sitting back against the tree with his knees drawn up and talking with a calmness and seriousness which aroused the wrath of old Trimmer. "It's a kind of an interesting situation. We have as much right on the scow as the land has, as I see it—"

"Sure, you learn that in the third grade!" shouted Pee-wee. "That's logic."

"Really, the best thing to do," drawled Townsend, "would be to remove the land, which would let us down onto the scow and that would let you out of the difficulty. We'd be answerable to the owner of the scow."

"It belonged to the big dredge," Pee-wee said excitedly. "I knew all the men on that dredge; I used to hang out on that dredge; those men were all friends of mine. We wouldn't be trespassing except your land is in the way."

"If you want us to shovel the land out of here we'll do it," suggested Roly Poly.

"Then the tree'll fall over," said Brownie.

"Gee whiz," shouted Pee-wee, "it'll serve the tree right because all the time fellers are being accused of trespassing in apple trees and now you can see for yourself that apple trees are just as bad. They trespass on scows."

"We could have this tree fined ten dollars," said Billy, "if we wanted to report it to the dredging company in New York."

"Or it would have to go to jail for thirty days," yelled Pee-wee.

"I don't see what we're going to do, Mr. Trimmer," said Townsend.

"I know what we're going to do," said Pee-wee; "we're going to do a lot of things. We're natives of this island."

"We don't recognize this land," said Townsend; "we consider it beneath us."

"Sure it's beneath us!" shouted Pee-wee.

"It simply happens to trespass on the scow first," said Townsend. "I think we'll stand on our rights."

"Well, yer ain't goin' ter stand on my property, yer ain't!" old Trimmer bellowed, his wrath rising. Townsend's calmness seemed to goad him to a perfect frenzy.

"Well, then," said Townsend, "the only thing for us to do is to shovel out a space and camp on that. Then our feet will be on the scow—"

"We'll be on friendly territory," shouted Pee-wee. "Your land can camp here with us if it wants to."

"Or you can take it away, just as you please," said Townsend. "Only we warn you not to take any liberties with this scow. We're personally acquainted with Mr. Steam of the Steam Dredging Company and we're going to charter this scow, now that we're on it. We can get another desert island to put on it if necessary."

"Do you see this traffic sign?" Pee-wee yelled at the top of his voice. He stood like some conquering hero, holding the martial stop sign with one hand. "The bottom of this bar is planted on the scow. Do you hear the noise it makes when I bump it up and down? It goes right through this land. We take possession of this scow in the name of the new Alligator Patrol or maybe it'll be the Turtles, we don't know yet. We plant our banner on the—the—"

"The rye bread," said Billy.

"And if this land," Pee-wee continued, "that used to be a peninsula and stuck out over the river from your field and trespassed on the scow when it didn't have any right to because it wasn't friends with the dredge men—if this land wants to stay here it can."

"What do you say, Mr. Trimmer?" Townsend laughed. "If you want to tow this whole business back up to your place we'll help you shovel the land off the scow. We don't want to camp on an island that violates the law. But you haven't got anything to do with this scow. I'm not asking you how it got alongside your field or why the dredging people didn't take it away when they took the dredge away; that's your business," he added rather significantly. "We'll admit the land is yours—"

"No, we won't!" said Pee-wee.

"Yes, we will," said Townsend quietly. "Now what do you want to do about this property? Shall we wrap it up for you or shall we send it? Our dealings are with the steam dredge people. Now what do you say? By the way, will you have a cruller?"

It was perfectly evident that Townsend Ripley, with rather more quiet shrewdness than any of them had given him credit for, had gently stabbed Mr. Trimmer in a weak spot. It was the scow that old Trimmer wanted. How he had come by it had been only faintly suggested by Townsend. How it had chanced to be moored in that secluded spot under the projecting land after the big dredge had gone away, was not discussed and is not a part of this story. It seemed evident that old Trimmer was rather disturbed at the thought of the boys getting in touch with the dredge people.

"Go ahead n' camp on it then," he said in sulky surrender; "and don't make a nuisance of yourselves writin' letters to the dredging company. Them men has got something else ter do besides bothering with a crew of crazy youngsters."

"But you know what you said about trespassing, Mr. Trimmer," said Townsend. "You have taught us that we shouldn't trespass and we thank you for the lesson. We'll have to drop Mr. Steam a line. How about a cruller, Mr. Trimmer? They were just stolen from our small friend's kitchen. Don't care for stolen fruit, hey? You're too particular, Mr. Trimmer."

CHAPTER XV

LIFE ON THE UNKNOWN SHORE

Seldom has there been a surrender so complete and unconditional. There were no banners to celebrate the triumph (for which Pee-wee took all the credit) but as old Trimmer started up the river Pee-wee turned the sign so that the word GO faced the departing voyager like a commanding finger to order the vanquished from his victorious presence.

"Do you think he had some treasure in the scow?" Pee-wee asked. "Maybe if we dig we'll find some gold nuggets."

"Let's try some of those cocoanut nuggets," said Townsend.

"Didn't I know how to handle him?" said Pee-wee. "Now the island is ours, isn't it?"

"I think before we have supper," said Townsend, "we'll write a line to the dredging people. What do you say?"

"We'll write it on bark from the tree on account of our being wild and uncivilized," said Pee-wee. "I can make ink out of prune juice and we can write with a stick like hunters do when they get lost."

"Do they carry prune juice with them?" Billy asked.

"Sometimes they use blood," said Pee-wee. "I can make ink from onions too—invisible ink. Shall I make some?"

"I thought you were going to make a hunter's stew," said Brownie.

"Go ahead," said Roly Poly, "you make the hunter's stew —it won't be invisible, will it?"

"It will when we get through with it," said Billy.

"And while you're making the stew, Rip will write the letter and the first one of us that goes ashore will mail it."

The letter which Townsend Ripley wrote to the dredging company asking permission to use the old scow surmounted by a luxurious desert island was very funny, but it was not nearly as funny as the hunter's stew which Pee-wee made.

Their minds now free as to their rights (at least, for the time being) they sprawled about under the little tree as the afternoon sunlight waned and partook of the weird concoction which Pee-wee cooked in the dishpan over the rough fireplace which they had constructed. And if Pee-wee was not the equal of his friend Roy Blakeley in the matter of cooking, he was at least vastly superior to him in the matter of eating, and as he himself observed, "Gee whiz, eating is more important than cooking anyway."

It was pleasant sitting about on this new and original

desert island which combined all the attractions of wild life with substantial safety. Only its overlapping edges could wash away and as these melted and disappeared the island gradually assumed a square and orderly conformation; its bleak and lonely coast formed a tidy square and looked like some truant back yard off on a holiday. What it lost in rugged grandeur it made up in modern neatness and seemed indeed a desert Island with all improvements.

Nestling within its stalwart and water-tight timbers it presented a scene of varied beauty. Grasshoppers disported gayly upon its rugged surface, occasionally leaping inadvertently into the surrounding surf and kicking their ungainly legs in the sparkling water.

A pair of adventurous robins that had refused to desert the fugitive peninsula were chirping in the little blossom-laden tree and one of them came down and perched upon the traffic sign to prune his feathers before retiring. Savage beetles roamed wild over the isle, and wild angleworms, disturbed by the late upheaval, squirmed about in quest of new homes.

The vegetation on the island appeared in gay profusion, reminding one of the Utopian scenes of fragrant beauty which delighted the eyes of the bold explorers who first landed on the shores of Florida.

Yellow dandelions dotted the greensward, purple violets peeped up through the overgrown grass, and a rusty tin can, memento of some prehistoric fisherman perhaps, lay near the shore. Not even the geometrical perfection of the island detracted from its primitive and rugged beauty.

True, it had no bays or wooded coves where pirates might

have lurked, and it was fickle to any one spot. But wheresoever its wanton fancy took it the dying sunlight flickered down through the little tree and glazed the spotless blossoms so full of promise that clustered above the little band of hardy adventurers.

Before they had finished their repast—a repast as strange and surprising as the island itself—they had drifted half a mile upstream with the incoming tide. Here the sturdy underpinning of the desert isle caught upon a tiny reef and the island swung slowly around like a sleepy carrousel and rested from its travels.

CHAPTER XVI

BEFORE THE PARTY

Meanwhile we must return to the mother country, to take note of important happenings there. While our doughty explorers were eating their hunter's stew in this strange land and sprawling beneath their tree in the gathering twilight surrounded by unknown perils, the gay Silver Fox Patrol returned from New York after a day spent in shopping and sightseeing.

They proceeded at once to their railroad car down by the river where they found the Ravens, who had just returned from a hike. Soon the Elks, returning from an auto ride, joined their comrades and a lively discussion occurred. It pertained to the lawn party to be given that evening at the home of Miss Minerva Skybrow of the Camp-fire Girls.

"What time do you have supper at your house?" Doc Carson asked Roy Blakeley.

"We have it about eight o'clock on Saturdays," said Roy. "My father's playing golf."

"Same here," said Artie Van Arlen; "my father has to stay late so as to beat your father."

"If he stays at the links long enough to do that you'll never see him again," said Roy. "What time is this racket supposed to be, anyway?"

"Eight sharp," said Grove Bronson.

"Are we going to go all separated together or all separated at once?" Roy asked.

"Positively," said Warde Hollister.

"Positively what?" asked Connie Bennett.

"It's all the same to me, only different," said Roy. "Only this is what I was thinking. We all have supper at different times except Pee-wee and he has supper all the time. As Abraham Lincoln said at the battle of Marne, 'Some people are half hungry all the time, some people are all hungry half the time, but Pee-wee is *all* hungry *all* the time.' I wonder where he is anyway?"

"Down in Bennett's having a soda, I guess," said Westy Martin.

"Is he going to the party?" Tom Warner asked.

"Search me," said Westy. "I guess not, he doesn't dance. I heard somebody say he was with some fellows up the river."

"Starting a new bunch of patrols, I suppose," said Roy.

"Bentley's gardener saw him somewhere," said Wig Weigand.

"It's just possible he was somewhere," said Roy. "I've

Percy Keese Fitzhugh

often known him to go there. Let's talk of something pleasant. What do you say we get a light supper down here. Anybody that wants to go home and dress can do it only he has to hustle. She wants us to wear our scout suits anyway, she said so. I say let's get a few eats down here and then wash up and all hike it up there together. United we stand—"

"What are we going to eat?" Grove Bronson asked. "I don't see anything here but some fishhooks and a package of tacks."

"Listen to the voice from Pee-wee's old patrol!" said Roy. "*Eats*! I'll fry some killies. Haven't we got some milk chocolate and Ulika biscuits? I bet there's a large crowd of peanuts and other junk in Pee-wee's locker. Can't you wait till you get to Minerva's? She'll have chicken salad and ice cream and sandwiches and cake and lemonade and paper napkins and souvenirs and everything. We'll feel more like eating a little later. What do you all say? If each of us goes home we'll never get together again; we'll all straggle in there one by two."

"Suppose she doesn't have anything but a couple of fancy boxes of bonbons; you know how girls are," said Doc Carson. "Safety first, that's what I say."

"I haven't had anything to eat since lunch time," said Ralph Warner.

"Minerva wouldn't wish anything like that on us," said Connie.

"You said it," said Roy; "they're not passing around famines up at her house. Where do you think we're going? To Russia? Minerva's got the Sandwich Islands green with envy. What's the use of spoiling refreshments by eating now? You fellows are worse than the children of Armenia! I say, let's have a swim; the tide is nice and high, and then rest up and eat some crackers and hike up to the party. They'll be throwing chocolate cake at us up there.

"My patrol all have their good suits on; most of the rest of you have some Christmas tree regalia in your lockers, and the others can beat it home and hurry up back. What do you say? Aye, aye, aye, aye, aye, aye, aye, aye!" Roy shouted. "Carried by a large majority! Come on, let's go in for a swim while the tide's up. That will help to give us an appetite."

"What do you mean, 'help to give us one?'" asked Artie Van Arlen. "Haven't I got four already?"

"Well, when you come out of the water you'll have five," said Roy.

"Suppose—suppose," said Dorry Benton, who was ever cautious, "suppose, just *suppose* they should only have lady fingers and grape juice, or something like that." He stood uncertain, dangling his bathing suit. "Suppose they should have afternoon tea crackers. Did you ever eat those?"

"They're more likely to have roast turkey," said Roy. "Don't I go up there every couple of days and play tennis? I can't play the game even because they're always pushing a chunk of cake into my left hand."

"I know, Roy," said Warde Hollister. He also was a far-sighted and thoughtful boy who did his homework in the afternoon and started on New Year's saving up for next

Christmas. "But this is a lawn-party—Japanese napkins and lettuce and things like that. We're taking an awful chance, Roy. We may get salted almonds—"

"You should worry," said Roy; "here's your bathing suit. Come on, we've only got about an hour. Think of the poor children of Europe. Minerva Skybrow is positively guaranteed. I never saw such a bunch, you're always worrying about something."

And with that, by way of starting things, he pushed Connie Bennett into the water...

CHAPTER XVII

THE SCENE IS SET

In history we read that while the hardy pioneers toiled and suffered in the New England forest the gay votaries of fashion danced and made merry in the royal courts of Europe. And history repeats itself, for while Minerva Skybrow and her girl companions decked the Skybrow lawn with lanterns of many colors, and frilled their hair, and festooned the rustic summer-house with streamers, the sturdy adventurers who swore allegiance to the martial traffic sign of Pee-wee Harris were suffering as no hardy pioneer had ever suffered before as they loyally partook of the hunter's stew which their leader had prepared in the dishpan. If, indeed, this novel concoction was the favorite fare of hunters, it is no wonder that the race of hunters is becoming extinct. But our business is not with the explorers.

The spacious lawn of the Skybrow home was bathed in the soft light of many paper lanterns depending from cords strung from tree to tree. Other lanterns nestled in the spreading trees like jewels in a setting of foliage.

On that night the genial moon smiled down upon the Camp-fire Girls and sent his myriad of rays like a

Percy Keese Fitzhugh

serenading party to enliven the festive scene. The place looked like some enchanted grove. A platform had been built for the dancing, several little khaki-colored tents that had done service in the North Woods (north of Bridgeboro) dotted the lawn, the emblem of the Campfire Girls waved above the summer-house, bathed in the glow of a small search-light, and, glory of glories, a small tent nestling under a spreading elm near the moonlit river contained a table which looked like a snowy monument reared in tribute to the god of food.

Yes, Roy was right; the Skybrows did not do these things by halves. Here indeed was a haven for the famished; here rescue awaited the starving scout. In the center stood a pyramid of triangular sandwiches, rivalling in magnitude the pyramids of Egypt. This was flanked by two gorgeous icing cakes, one white and one brown. A bowl of chicken salad overflowed its cut glass confines, the same as Pee-wee's island had overflowed its trusty scow.

It is true that the much feared salted almonds were there but they crouched in shame under the spreading sides of a wooden hash-bowl camouflaged with crepe paper and piled with jellied doughnuts. If there were any lady fingers they did not show their faces (if lady fingers have faces) but the jovial raspberry tart was there in all its glory a hundred strong.

"Oh, I think everything is perfectly *scrumptious*," said Minerva Skybrow, completing a tour of inspection at this culinary paradise and allowing herself an olive or two.

"Goodness gracious, let them alone or there won't be any left," said Miss Dora Dane Daring.

"Silly!" said Minerva. "There are *oceans* of them. Doesn't

the river look perfectly lovely in the moonlight?"

"Oh, I think everything is *perfectly adorable*," said another friend; "and the weather is just *heavenly*. For goodness' sakes, let the candy alone; that's the fourth piece you took."

"Listen," said Minerva. "I'm not going to let a *single one* of them come out here till they have all arrived. We're going to have the concert in the house first and they've *just got* to listen to Mrs. Wild speak about the Camp-fire movement, because she's just *perfectly wonderful*. Do you know, I wish I had put the refreshments in the summer house. No, I don't either—yes, I do. It would have been more romantic—*rustic*."

"Oh, I think this tent is *perfect*," said another girl, slyly helping herself to a salted almond.

"I know," said Minerva, her hand stealing unconsciously toward a box of marsh mallows, "I know, but what I wanted was something unusual—symbolic. A rustic platform in one of the big trees would have been nice; it would have been sort of—sort of *scoutish*. I want to have things *different*. That's why boys always make fun of the Camp-fire Girls, they think we're *tame*. Think how Roy Blakeley and his friends actually camped in that adorable old railroad car while it was traveling, goodness knows where. When I went to the Aero Club reception with Harold Fall they had the refreshments in a great balloon; we had to go up to it on a ladder—*shh*, listen! Did you hear a noise?"

A chorus of excited whisperings followed her startled query.

"No, where?"

"What was it?"

"Was it a voice?"

"You mean on the river?"

"*Shh*, listen," said Minerva; "*look*, do you see a light—right there among the bushes? *Shh*. Don't run."

There was indeed a light shining through the dark foliage alongshore and presently a voice was to be heard, a voice speaking words to strike terror to the stoutest Camp-fire Girl heart.

"I watched for the cops," it said, "and as soon as I saw them I beat it across the field and told the gang and every one got away but it was a narrow escape. One detective had me by the collar. *This is going to be easy though.*"

"Bandits!" whispered Minerva.

"They're going to rob the house while we're on the lawn," breathed Margaret Timerson.

"They're crouching on the shore just behind those bushes," said another girl.

"Leave it to me," said the mysterious voice. "I'll handle them."

CHAPTER XVIII

EVERY WHICH WAY

We left Merry-go-round Island revolving gracefully upon a tiny reef whence it was borne by the rising tide. We are now to take up our narrative at the point where the island ceased spinning and was carried slowly on upstream by the incoming waters. When the tide reached flood, the island hesitated upon the still water, then like some obedient and clumsy ox, moved slowly downstream again upon the ebb. And meanwhile, the day departed and darkness fell upon the winding river and the hardy adventurers lit their lanterns.

"I was hoping we might stick in some pleasant spot," said Townsend, "where the fishing is good. I forgot how a floating island might act in a tidal river. I wish this island would make up its mind to something. Just when I want to explore the western coast I find it's the eastern coast. I don't know where I'm at—"

"You don't have to know where you're at to have fun," said Pee-wee.

"I know it," said Townsend; "but when I hike fifteen or twenty feet to the north coast of the island and then the island swings around and I find I'm on the south coast, I've got to hike all the way across the island again to get to the north coast and when I get there I find I'm on the west coast. Then I cross to the east coast and in about a minute I find I'm on the southern shore.

"No matter where I go I'm somewhere else; it's discouraging. I've walked forty-eleven miles since supper trying to keep on the western coast and here I am on the north—wait a minute—the eastern coast. If this Island won't stay still I can't explore it."

"I tell you what we can do," said Pee-wee; "we can penetrate the interior, then we'll always be in the same place."

So they penetrated the interior and sprawled on the ground and chatted.

"When we find another member," said Pee-wee, "we'll have a full patrol and then we'll have to start a scout record and write down a description of the island and everything we see, because scouts have to do that because they have to be observant and they have to be accurate when they describe things."

"Would you say that this little tree is near the west coast of the island?" Townsend asked. "I've followed it around for the last half hour and I don't know where it is except it's here."

"Here isn't a place," said Roly Poly.

"Sure it is," shouted Pee-wee; "here is just as much a place as there."

"More," said Townsend. "There are three places—here, there, and everywhere; I've often heard them spoken of."

"That's just where this island is," said Brownie.

"Absolutely," said Townsend, "only it won't stay there. Is there anything more we can eat? Anything more that you don't have to *make*? My long tramp in search of the west coast has made me hungry again."

"I can make flapjacks," said Pee-wee; "I've got eight pounds of Indian meal."

"How far would I have to hike to digest them?" Townsend asked.

"You'd need a bigger island than this," said Brownie. "You couldn't digest a flapjack on anything smaller than South America."

"Give me a piece of chocolate," said Townsend, "and a couple of prunes."

"It looks nice up the river in the moonlight, doesn't it?" Brownie asked.

"You mean down the river," said Townsend.

"I'm facing—"

"Don't try to find out where you're facing," said Townsend. "Here, eat a prune."

"I'm going to turn in pretty soon," said Nuts.

"That's a new place to turn," said Townsend. "We've

turned everywhere but *in*. In the morning we'll turn out; then we will have turned everywhere."

"We're flopping downstream pretty fast," said Brownie; "that's one sure thing."

"I'm glad there's something sure," said Townsend. It was as good as a circus to see him sitting against the tree with his knees drawn up, glancing this way and that with a funny look of patient resignation on his face.

"What do you say we put the tent up in the heart of the interior? Then we'll be able to find it in the morning. The unknown heart of the interior seems to be the only place we can be sure of. At least it always stays inside. Hand me that grocery box from the extreme southern shore, will you? And another prune? The heart of my interior demands another prune. Do you know, Discoverer, what I think? I think I see a settlement. I don't know where it is because I don't know which way I'm facing, but I'm certainly facing a settlement—or at least I was a second ago. There it is again. I think we're nearing the coast of Japan; I see a Japanese lantern. That's funny. Did we pass the Philippines?"

"I don't know," said Brownie. "We passed Corbett's Lumber Yard."

"The Philippines are farther along," said Townsend; "they're the second turn to our left. If this island hits Japan they'll grab it; I have a feeling that they'll grab it like the island of Yap."

"*I've got an inspiration! I've got an inspiration!*" shouted Pee-wee in a voice of thunder. "I know where we're at. That's Mr. Skybrow's place down there. He owns a lot of railroads and things! They're having a lawn party there to-night!"

"Are they having anything to eat?" Townsend asked quietly.

"Yum, yum—m-m-m!" said Pee-wee. "They have everything. Once I went to Minerva's birthday party and I couldn't go to school all next week, that's how much they have to eat there. Get the clothes-sticks. Get the clothes-sticks! Let's pole the island to shore. I bet she'll like you because you're big—I'll introduce you to her—all my old troop is going to be there—hurry up—push—keep pushing!"

"Reach over to the west coast and hand me that pole from the north coast before it goes over to the east coast," said Townsend quietly.

"Get up! *Get up!*" shouted Pee-wee, all excitement. "Aren't you going to get up?"

"Positively," said Townsend, dragging himself to his feet.

"Shh!" said Pee-wee, "let's surprise them."

"You're the only one that's making any noise," said Townsend.

"I mean myself, too," said Pee-wee. "Shhhh."

"He's telling himself to keep still," Brownie, unable to control his laughter.

"I mean all of us—me too," said Pee-wee. "Shh."

It was during the long and rather difficult process of poling the island to shore that Pee-wee, unable to impose more than comparative quiet upon himself, edified his companions with an account of his recent adventure in Barrel Alley.

And it was his seemingly ominous mention of "cops" and fugitives which Minerva Skybrow and her friends, lingering at the little refreshment tent near the river, overheard. At that moment the desert island was bobbing against the thick rhododendron bushes at the edge of the lawn.

CHAPTER XIX

THE EARTHLY PARADISE

"I don't care who it is or what it is," said Dora Dane Daring; "I'm not afraid of the biggest bandit that ever lived. I'm going to find out what those men are doing lurking about here."

Without another word she strode forward, parted the rhododendron bushes, and confronted the marauders.

"Well, I—*never*—in—*all* my *life*," she cried. "It's little Walter Harris! What on *earth* are you doing here?"

"I discovered this island," said Pee-wee; "we're exploring it. One of these fellers is a native because he was on it before it was an island."

"Look out you don't get your feet wet on the stern and rock-bound coast," said Townsend. "Hold the lantern, Brownie."

"Did you ever *see* such a thing!" said Minerva Skybrow, emerging through the bushes, accompanied by her official staff. "Walter Harris, what in goodness' name are you doing here? I thought you were robbers. What in *all creation* are you up to? And how did you happen to get here?"

"We've been going around quite a little lately," said Townsend quietly.

"This is Townsend Ripley," said Pee-wee; "he's a friend of mine; these fellers are all friends of mine. We're exploring."

"We're very glad to meet you, Mr. Ripley," said Minerva, while Miss Daring whispered in the ear of Miss Timerson, "Isn't he nice? So tall."

"We thought we'd come to the party," said Pee-wee.

"Have you any parking space for islands?" Townsend asked.

"Oh, *indeed* we have," said Minerva, "and you're going to be the star guests. May we step on the island?"

"Yes, indeed, it's very steady," said Townsend, helping them one after another onto the frowning coast while Brownie held the lantern. "Wherever we go we take our island with us; it's like ivory soap, it floats. Will you have a piece of wild chocolate, out of the heart of the interior?"

"Isn't he just *lovely*," whispered Miss Daring.

"So can we stay?" asked Pee-wee.

"Stay? I wouldn't let you go for anything," said Minerva. "Listen, girls, I've got an *inspiration*—"

"I have lots of those," said Pee-wee.

"They grow wild here," said Townsend.

"Listen," said Minerva, "I have a perfectly *marvellous* idea."

She sat down on the grocery box and in her joy and excitement fairly drowned out Pee-wee who was struggling with a vehement running narrative of the day's adventures.

"Oh, it will be simply *divine*," said Minerva. "Listen—don't interrupt me—I'm going to have the refreshments served on this island. I'm going to have the old painter's scaffold for a *gang-plank* leading to it—"

"There are refreshments then?" Townsend asked quietly.

"Refreshments? Aren't you perfectly *terrible*! Of course there are—*oceans* of them."

"No more oceans for me," said Townsend. "Hereafter I'm going to live on shore. My sailing—flopping—days are over."

"You're too funny for anything," said Minerva. "Listen, do you see that little tent? The refreshments are all in there. There's just time before the guests all come to move everything over here. I want you boys to help me. We're going to call it the *dessert island* instead of the *desert island*. Isn't that adorable? Isn't it odd? Everyone will go into raptures over it, you see if they don't. You'll let us use your island, won't you?"

"We'll make you a present of it," said Townsend.

"My idea," said Miss Timerson, "would be to tie it to

these bushes that stick out over the water. It ought to be far enough away from the—the mainland—to be romantic. How far away do you think it should be, Mr. Ripley?"

"The way I feel about it I think it should be at least two thousand miles off."

"Silly!" said Miss Daring. "Please be serious. Do you think about three yards would be romantic?"

"I never measured romance by the yard," said Townsend, "but I should think about three yards and a half of romance would be enough. If we have any left over we can give it to the discoverer. He eats it alive."

"And I'll tell you what I'll do," shouted Pee-wee; "it's an inspiration."

"Another?" Townsend asked.

"I'll—I'll—I'll stay on the island—"

"I thought so," said Townsend.

"And—and—I'll stand right here by the traffic sign and after somebody that's eating has had enough, I'll turn the sign so it says STOP; I'll turn it so it's facing him."

"Did you ever hear anything so absurd?" said Minerva.

"I think it would be picturesque," said Dora.

"And sensible, too," said Margaret, "because some of those scouts will just stay here and gorge themselves and won't dance at all."

"I think it's a very good idea," said Townsend; "it will relieve congestion here. A food traffic cop."

"I'll be it," shouted Pee-wee.

"Where is this romantic scaffold?" Townsend asked.

"The painters left it in the cellar," said Minerva. "Let's hurry, I'll show you where it is."

There was, indeed, just time enough to arrange this novel life-saving station with its picturesque gang-plank before the guests began to arrive.

"And this is the end of our wild adventures on a foreign shore," said Townsend, as he carried one end of the old scaffold across the dim-lighted lawn accompanied by the group of excited maidens; "we wind up at a lawn party. This is what the discoverer has brought us to."

"Don't you think he's just *killing*?" Minerva asked.

"More than that," said Townsend; "his hunter's stew is more than killing. Did you ever try any of it?"

"Never mind, you're going to have some delicious chicken salad," said Minerva.

The boys, under Minerva's enthusiastic supervision, tied the island about six feet from shore. The romantic gang-plank kept it from drifting closer in while two clothes-poles driven into the bottom of the river just below it prevented it from drifting with the ebbing tide. Pee-wee's trusty clothesline was stretched between the little apple tree and the overhanging rhododendron bushes as an auxiliary mooring and to hold the island steady.

Thus secured and free from the prosaic shore, the romantic isle presented an inviting scene, with the little tent upon it and Japanese lanterns shedding a mellow light from the bushes and the securing clothesline. The rippling water flickered with a gentle and undulating glow and inverted paper lanterns could be seen reflected beneath the surface, as if indeed the beholder could look down and see romantic and picturesque Japan on the opposite side of the earth.

The scaffold, forgetting its prosy usage, was resplendent in a winding robe of bunting and on its railing where cans of white lead and linseed oil had disported hung lanterns of every color in the rainbow. To this enchanted isle would stroll dance-weary couples and famishing scouts to regale themselves in this dim, detached, earthly paradise.

"Wait a minute, oh, just wait a minute!" cried Minerva in the spell of such an inspiration as comes only once in a lifetime. "Oh, just wait *one minute*."

She hurried across the lawn, returning presently with a huge, spotless apron with strings of goodly dimension which, in a very glow of inspired joy, she tied around the waist of Pee-wee Harris. It was necessary to shorten it by a series of pokes and pushes by which it was tucked up under its own strings and lifted clear of the adventurous feet of the scout. Nor was that all, for somewhere out of the mysterious depths of the house, Minerva had brought a starched and snowy chef's cap with which she crowned our hero.

"You be right here when they begin coming down," Minerva said, "and stand close to the traffic sign and if any boy stays here too long turn the STOP sign on him."

"And turn it on yourself if necessary," said Townsend.

"I won't let anybody eat more than about—about—five helpings. That'll be enough for them, hey?" said Pee-wee.

"Goodness gracious, yes," said Dora Dane Daring.

"You're the steward, remember," said Minerva. "Do you know what a steward is?"

"He's—he's named after a stew," said Pee-wee, hitching up his spreading apron. "You leave the people to me, I'll handle them."

CHAPTER XX

GONE

The steward (or the stew, as Townsend thenceforth called him) did not attend the party. A preliminary tour of the grounds convinced him that adventures of his particular kind were not to be found there. Dancing was not in his line. Music (except the clamorous music of his own voice) he did not care for. And he did not care to hear what Mrs. Wild had to say about the Camp-fire movement.

To him the crucial part of the whole party was the eats and he lingered near them like a faithful sentinel. The artistic quality of these saved them from devastation. Those pyramids of luscious beauty could not be denied by human hands without showing the indubitable signs of vandalism. Their very splendor saved them.

It is true that he skilfully extracted an olive from the symmetrical mound of chicken salad and took an almond and a macaroon and other detached dainties that were not made sacred and secure by their own architecture. But for the most part Pee-wee was faithful to his trust. He knew his time would come. And then, oh, then, that proud tower of interlaced sandwiches would look like Rheims Cathedral.

Thus an hour passed and the merry throng emerged upon the lawn and made a direct assault upon the dancing platform, lured by strains of irresistible music. Some strolled about but none out of the radius of that melodious magnetism, and Pee-wee remained undisturbed on the romantic isle of eats.

He sat upon the edge of the island, the extreme western coast, fishing for eels, with a string, a bent pin and a salted almond. It seemed that the eels did not care for salted almonds, so Pee-wee endeavored to tempt them with a chocolate bonbon but the bonbon dissolved on the pin, forming a sort of subterranean chocolate sundae, and the eels ignored it.

"I bet I know what's the matter," said Pee-wee; "they're afraid to come near the island on account of the lights." At all events the eels appeared to shun the neighborhood of the party; they were not in society.

Just then Pee-wee had an inspiration. In the light of its consequences it was probably the most momentous inspiration that he ever had. "I know what I'll do," he said. "I'll use a long, long stick that'll reach way, way, way out." And he glanced about him in quest of a "long, long stick" with which to beguile the bashful eels. His inquiring eye lit upon one of the long clothes-line supporters which Townsend had driven into the river bottom to help hold the island in position.

It is necessary to understand the strategical position of this prospective fishing rod. These two poles had been forced down into the muddy bottom just south of the island and the southern edge of the island lay against them and was thus prevented from drifting down with the ebbing tide. The makeshift gang-plank, gay with bunting,

Percy Keese Fitzhugh

held the island off shore and the ropes between the island and the bushes steadied it. This crude engineering was quite sufficient. BUT—

There is a church somewhere in Europe of which it is said that if a certain brick were removed the whole edifice would fall in ruins. Pee-wee was not even an amateur engineer. That world-stirring consequences could flow from an act so casual and trivial as securing a fishing rod never entered his innocent and pre-occupied mind. He did not know that in the hasty calculations of Townsend all the component parts of this system of props and fetters were necessary one to another. He removed the brick and the cathedral fell and there followed a catastrophe compared to which the World War is a mere incident. If he had pulled the north pole out of the earth the sequel could hardly have been more momentous.

Sublimely innocent of the fact that he was unhinging the universe, Pee-wee arose, advanced to the outer pole and began tugging on it. It did not come up easily for the force of the rapidly ebbing tide caused the island to press against it like a brake. But he succeeded at last and as he dragged the muddy pole across the grass, the island turned slowly cornerwise to the shore.

In his preoccupation, Pee-wee did not notice this. He tied his fishline to the end of the pole, bent another pin and provisioned it with a stuffed olive, requisitioned from a cutglass dish nearby. How he intended to support this lengthy pole so that its end might reach the neighborhood of the coy eels is not a part of this narrative for Pee-wee's angling enterprise never reached that point.

He was presently startled by a splash and looking around he saw that the end of the scaffold had slipped off the island. He was now aroused to the imminent peril of the Isle of Desserts and to the terrible responsibility which fell to the clothesline and the bushes.

As the island turned slowly outward the clothes-line strained but held fast. But the rhododendron bushes had not the same heroic quality. For a few moments they resisted, but the island, now at the mercy of the ebb, tugged and tugged, and presently a mass of bush gave up the struggle and came away, rope and all. The earthly paradise with its luscious store of cake and chicken salad, its commanding pyramid of sandwiches flanked by icing cakes, its plates of dates and olives and candy of every variety, its mound of jellied doughnuts, and a mammoth freezer full of ice cream, floated majestically down the moonlit river, trailing a huge clump of rhododendron bush after it like the tail of a comet.

CHAPTER XXI

FOILED

And now out of the still and moonlit night arose peal after peal of thunder imparting a note of terror to this world catastrophe. Never before had the thunderous voice of our hero rent the heavens as it did now.

"Help! Help! I'm floating away with the eats."

It is no wonder that the man in the moon smiled at what he saw on the river that night. Seeing the laden board, the pyramid of sandwiches rearing its luscious pinnacle toward heaven, he seemed to wink at Pee-wee—with what purport who shall say? Sufficient that our hero saw him not.

"*He-e-e-elp!* I'm drifting downstream with the refreshments," he called. "*He-e-elp!*"

They heard him amid their revels. Townsend Ripley who had suffered the assaults of the hunter's stew heard him. The scouts who had eaten a "light supper" heard him. Warde Hollister who had pled with Roy for a safety first policy heard him. Minerva Skybrow heard him and paused aghast in the midst of a two-step. For what was a two-step now compared to the one-step which Pee-wee had taken? Roly Poly and Brownie, also victims of the hunter's stew, heard him as they waited patiently, and were struck dumb with terror. Only the man in the moon smiled, and winked at Pee-wee.

"*He-e-e-e-e-el-l-l-p! I'm floating away with the eats!*"

But did he really need any help?

They rushed to the shore pell-mell and some hurried to the barn for the only means of rescue—an old disused skiff and a leaky, discarded canoe. Others gazed in wistful silence out upon the glinting water.

"*Hurry! Hurry!*" cried Minerva. "I can see it! Don't you see the lanterns down there?"

"He's on the flats, I think," said Warde.

"He's on the table," shouted Roy.

"He's in the channel!"

"He's in the ice cream!"

"Listen, he's calling!"

"His mouth is full, I can't hear him."

"*Hurry! Hurry! Oh, hurry!*" cried Minerva.

"I'll tell you what let's do," Roy said.

"You told us once," said Warde; "that's enough."

"I saved the ice cream freezer from rolling off," shouted Pee-wee.

"A lot of good that does us," shouted Doc Carson.

"Put it where it will be safe," shouted Townsend.

"All right, I will," shouted Pee-wee.

"Gracious goodness, he isn't going to eat it, is he?" Margaret Timerson asked.

"He'll have to finish whatever else he's eating first," said Doc Carson. "Push that boat off, we have only a minute to act in."

"How long does it usually take him to finish a sandwich?" Minerva asked.

"Three-tenths of a second," said Roy.

"He'll be too frightened to eat," said Dora Daring.

"He's never too frightened to eat," said Connie Bennett.

"He consumes pie while he's consumed with fear," Roy said.

"He consumes everything," said Warde.

"Oh, what will we ever *do*?" Minerva walled, wringing her arms in desperation.

"The thing to do is to reach him before he gets really started," said Doc Carson, who was ever thoughtful and far-sighted. "When he starts he works fast. I don't think he's really begun yet. He believes in fair play and he wouldn't start before ten o'clock—that's refreshment time, isn't it?"

"It was to be," said Minerva.

"That's the time we were waiting for," said Brownie.

"Has he a watch?" Margaret asked.

"Yes, it's usually about twenty minutes fast," said Roy.

"Oh, isn't that perfectly *terrible*!" said Dora.

"He'll make terrible inroads on it," said Connie Bennett.

"*Inroads*!" said Roy. "You mean turnpikes and highways."

"Well, then, why don't you boys hurry?" Minerva asked excitedly. "It isn't too late. *Oh, do hurry*!"

"We can never tow that island back against the tide," said Dorry Benton.

"We can remove the stuff to the boat though," said Artie Van Arlen.

"I'm going to 'phone to Mr. Speeder to get his motor-boat and go after him; he can tow it back."

"Listen—*shh*—he's calling," said Townsend.

"Shh—*shhhh*!"

"Listen."

Percy Keese Fitzhugh

From down the river, a little farther than before, came a voice spent by the distance. "*I'm on the flats, I'm stuck.*"

"Thank goodness!" said Minerva. "Now we can reach him."

"Are you going around?" Townsend shouted.

"The sandwiches are all falling down," called the voice. "The doughnuts are rolling out."

"Save them," shouted Roy.

"All right, I will," screamed Pee-wee.

"*Oh, such a relief,*" said Minerva. "Do you think he's stuck fast?"

"We can only hope," said Townsend. "Come on, let's hustle."

Words cannot describe the haste and excitement with which the skiff was launched and manned by a little band of doughty pioneers. Roy, Warde Hollister and Townsend Ripley were the crew, two rowing while the other steered.

"Can we help ourselves?" Warde asked, as they glided out on the river.

"Yes, yes, yes, help yourselves to *anything*," called Minerva, "only bring them back—pile them in the boat—it doesn't make any difference how—only hurry, he may drift off again."

"Now you see," said Roy, addressing Warde, "the harder you work and the longer you wait the hungrier you'll be.

Everything is working out fine, thanks to me."

"Oh, sure," said Warde, already breathless from his strenuous rowing, "they give you roast turkey up at Skybrows; they give you chicken salad and sandwiches and—only try to get it. I'm so hungry I could eat the island, thanks to you. I could eat a whisk-broom. Follow you and I'll starve."

"Did you ever eat any of that kid's hunter's stew?" Townsend asked as he rowed.

"Did we?" said Roy. "It's the best thing I know of if you want to stay home from school."

"It's kind of queer," said Townsend.

"Oh, yes, mysterious," said Warde.

"Let's talk of something pleasant," said Roy.

"Well, I'm pretty hungry, too," said Townsend.

"We'll soon be there," said Warde. "We had something of a scare, didn't we?"

"All's well that ends well," said Townsend.

"Oh, sure," said Roy, "only you don't end so *well* after eating hunter's stew. We should worry, we'll have all the stuff pretty soon now. Narrow escape, hey? *Oh, boy*, it would have been terrible to lose all that stuff. It looked like an altar, didn't it?"

"It'll look like a vacuum when we get through with it," said Warde.

"Do you think we can get it all in the boat?"

"If we can't, we'll tow the icing cakes behind," said Roy. "What *I'm* thinking fond thoughts about is the ice cream."

"Same here," said Townsend.

"Same here," said Warde.

And meanwhile the man in the moon winked down at Pee-wee.

CHAPTER XXII

IN THE GLARE OF THE SEARCH-LIGHT

Now the tide is a funny thing, especially in a small suburban river. The banks of a river being for the most part sloping, the river bed is narrower at the bottom than at the top. You don't have to wear glasses to see that. That is why the tide, as it recedes, runs faster and faster; because during the last hour or two of its recession it flows in narrower confines. This has been the settled policy of nature for many centuries, and it was so ordered for the benefit of Pee-wee Harris.

When the Merry-go-round Island floated leisurely against the Skybrow lawn the tide had been flowing out for about an hour. When this same rechristened island broke loose disguised as an earthly paradise, the tide was in a great hurry. And when the earthly paradise caught upon the flats the little remaining water was running as if it were going to catch a train.

Rapidly, ever so rapidly, the water slid down off the flats to join the hurrying water in the channel. And, presto, all of a sudden there was the Isle of Desserts high and dry surrounded by an ocean of oozy mud while the river, narrowed to a mere brook, rushed in its channel some

Percy Keese Fitzhugh

fifty feet distant. And there you are.

That is why the man in the moon (who knows all about the tides) winked at Pee-wee. At least, I suppose that is why he winked.

You could not have reached the Isle of Desserts with a boat or with snow-shoes or with stilts or with anything except an airplane. Swimming to it was out of the question. Shouting and screaming to it was feasible, of course. Radio operations were conceivable. But reach it no one could. The adventurer would have been swallowed in mud. This safe isolation would continue for a couple of hours and then the playful water would come rippling in again spreading a glinting coverlet over the flats once more and lifting the island upon its swelling bosom.

Down the narrowing river rowed our rescuing crew, and as they rowed the river narrowed. Soon the lantern light on the island was abreast of them, some forty or fifty feet distant.

"Hello, over there," called Warde.

"I'm pretty well," called Pee-wee.

"What are we going to do?" asked Townsend. "The tide has beat us to it. He's safe enough."

"Oh, he couldn't be safer," said Warde. "Our name is mud. All our rowing for nothing."

"How about the eats over there, Kid?" Warde called.

"They're all right," called Pee-wee, "only the ice cream is starting to melt. I stuck my finger in through the ice and the cream is kind of oozing out. Maybe I better eat it, hey? It won't hold out till the tide comes in. I ate a sandwich and that made me thirsty and I didn't want to be drinking the lemonade so I ate a piece of ice out of the freezer and that made me more thirsty so I drank some lemonade anyway and that made me hungry again and I'm going to eat a sardine sandwich only I'm afraid that'll make me thirsty and—"

"This is horrible," said Townsend; "it's like an endless chain. Where will the end be?"

"Do you think it would be all right for me to eat some chicken salad?" Pee-wee shouted. "The tide won't be high enough to float this island for two hours."

"Don't!" called Warde, stopping up his ears. "Have a heart."

"Have a what?" called Pee-wee.

"Have a doughnut," shouted Roy.

"All right," called Pee-wee. "There's some dandy cheese here in a kind of a little jar—*yum—yum*!"

"Don't!" shrieked Warde.

"Doughnut?" called Pee-wee.

"No, I said '*don't*'," called Warde. "You'll have me eating one of the oarlocks in a minute."

Soon a faint chugging could be heard; it ceased, presumably at the Skybrow lawn, then started again. Nearer and nearer it came until presently the racing boat of

Dashway Speeder came to a stop alongside them. Half a dozen girls and as many hungry male guests of the party were in it clamoring for news.

"This is terrible!" said Minerva. "I never *dreamed* of such a thing as this. Why, he's *marooned*!"

"I'm all safe," shouted Pee-wee, "don't you worry."

"*Safe*! I should think he is," said Dora. "If he had the British navy all around him he couldn't be safer."

"The world is at his feet," said Townsend.

"You mean at his mouth," said Roy.

"I never heard of such a thing in all my born days," said Margaret.

"He's cornered the food market," said another hungry guest.

"For goodness' sake turn your search-light on him, Dashway," said Minerva, "and let's see what he looks like. This is simply *tragic*."

Dashway Speeder turned the search-light of his launch across the fiats and there amid the surrounding mud, still bubbling from the effects of the departing tide, was presented a scene like unto a picture on a movie screen. There, bathed in light amid the surrounding gloom, like a film star in a disk of brightness, sat Scout Harris upon a grocery box surrounded by fallen sandwiches and with a goodly bowl securely held between his diminutive knees. It was a superb and mouth-watering close-up, to use the film phrase.

"I—I might as well eat some things, hey?" me lone voyager called. "Because it's past time for refreshments anyway and the tide won't carry me off for more than two hours and everybody'll be going home then and the ice cream is starting to melt, the lemon ice is getting all soft, so will it be all right to start eating the chicken salad and the sandwiches and things? I only kind of sort of tested them so far."

Warde Hollister stopped up his ears in an agony of torture while a dozen famishing boys flopped this way and that in attitudes of suffering despair.

"Yes, it will be all right," called poor Minerva in a kind of desperation. "It's the only thing, you might as well." She seemed resigned if not reconciled. "You might as well eat the ice cream anyway, it will only melt."

"And the chicken salad?" called the merciless hero, "and the sandwiches, too?"

"*Oh, this is too much,*" moaned Connie Bennett.

"It isn't so much as you might think," shouted Pee-wee.

"He must be hollow from head to foot," said Margaret.

"Yes, eat everything," wailed Minerva in the final spirit of utter resignation.

"Yum—yum," called Pee-wee. "Oh, boy, it's good."

And still the man in the moon winked down, and smiled his merry scout smile upon Scout Harris.

CHAPTER XXIII

THE DREAM OF KEEKIE JOE

On that night, in the back yard of Billy Gilson's tire repair shop, Keekie Joe, the sentinel of Barrel Alley, sat upon a pile of old Ford radiators, untangling a complicated mass of fishing-line. He was trying to follow a selected strand through the various fastnesses of the labyrinth.

The involved mass was really not a fishing-line but, in its untangled state, an apparatus for confounding and enraging pedestrians. Stretched across the sidewalk between two tin cans its function was to catch in the feet of passersby, thus pulling the clamorous cans about the ankles of the victim. Keekie Joe had always found this game diverting and he was wont to vary its surprises by filling the cans with muddy water.

But on this eventful night he was driven to dismantle the apparatus and consecrate it to a new use. For Keekie Joe was hungry and he dared not go home; so he was going fishing.

The hours following the crap game had not been golden hours for the sentinel of Barrel Alley. When he emerged from the tenement and rejoined Pee-wee after the episode of the crap game, he had ten cents that his father had given him with which to buy a package of cigarettes.

Keekie Joe was never able to consider consequences at a distance of more than ten minutes into the future. When he played hooky from school on Thursday it never occurred to him that he would be answerable to the powers that be on Friday. Notwithstanding that he was a sentinel he could never look ahead. And when Keekie Joe smoked several of his father's cigarettes on the way home, it never occurred to him that he would have to remain away from home through supper time, and until his father had retired for the night.

Thus it was that at nine o'clock or thereabouts, Keekie Joe realized that he was hungry and that four cigarettes stood between him and home, effectually barring the way. He measured the licking that he would get against the supper that he would get, and he decided to go fishing. No doubt his choice was well considered for the supper that he would get might not be a good one whereas the licking that he would get would be nothing short of magnificent.

Keekie Joe had not the slightest idea how to cook a fish and he could not think so far ahead as that. But food he must have. So he had dug some worms and put them in one of his trick cans and then proceeded to untangle the line. Having secured an unknotted length of five or six feet he equipped this with a fish-hook of his own manufacture and sallied forth toward the river. He was not only hungry, but sleepy, and it never occurred to him that this was the exorbitant price of four cigarettes.

Hunger and sleep vied with each other in the shuffling body of Keekie Joe as he crossed Main Street and cut across the fields toward the marshes.

Down by the river was a little shanty in which was a mass of fishing seine. It stood hospitably open, for the hinges of the door were all rusted away and the dried and shrunken boards lay on the marshy ground before the entrance. Keekie Joe had intended to make sure that there was nothing to eat in the shanty before casting his line in the neighboring water. For there was the barest chance that a petrified crust of bread, ancient remnant of some fisherman's lunch, might be in the place.

Once Keekie Joe had found such a crust there. But the place was bare now of everything except deserted spiderwebs, black and heavy with dust. These and the mass of net upon the ground were all that Keekie Joe could see in the light of the genial moonbeams which shone through the open doorway and wriggled in through the cracks in the weather-beaten boards.

And now again Keekie Joe had to make a choice. He was hungry, oh, so hungry. But he was sleepy, too, to the point of blinking half-consciousness. The eyes which had so often watched for "cops," and which had won for Keekie Joe his nickname, were half closed and he could hardly stand. Such a price for four cigarettes!

The eyes which had been so faithful to a doubtful trust and won the pay of an apple core, could not be trusted now to stay open while he sat, a ragged, lonely figure, on the shore dangling his line in quest of a morsel to eat. It was funny how these eyes, which had served others so well, seemed about to go back on their owner now. But so it was. And then, in a moment, a very strange thing happened.

As Keekie Joe leaned against the doorway blinking his eyes, he happened to look up at the moon and it seemed (probably because his eyes were blinking), it *seemed* as if the man in the moon winked at him, in a way shrewdly significant as if he might have something up his sleeve. Anyway, he could not keep his eyes open; sleep, for a little while at least, had triumphed over hunger and the faithful little sentinel of Barrel Alley stumbled over to the pile of net and sank down, exhausted, upon it.

And Keekie Joe dreamed a dream. A most outlandish dream. He dreamed that the licorice jaw-breaker which that strange boy had thrown at him was the size of a brick, and that as it fell upon the ground it broke into a thousand luscious fragments like the pane of plate-glass through which Keekie Joe had lately thrown a rock. He picked up the fragments and ate them, and there before him stood the strange, small boy, who threw a sponge cake directly at his head and hit him with it *plunk*. "Wotcher chuckin' dem at me fer?" Keekie Joe demanded menacingly.

But the small, strange boy (apparently without either fear or manners) scaled a pumpkin pie at him and said, "Do you think I'm scared of you?" He then squirted powdered sugar at him like poison gas and Keekie Joe toppled backward off the fence and could not watch for cops, because his eyes were full of powdered sugar. "Quit dat, d'yer hear!" he screamed. But the small, strange boy threw a ham straight at him and it fell on the ground with a thunderous crash and broke into a million thin slices with mustard on them.

The noise of this falling meteor awoke Keekie Joe and he sat up, holding the two sides of his head, startled and dizzy from hunger. And shining through the doorway of the shack he saw a light. It was not the moonlight, but another light, and he crept, light-headed and fearful, toward the opening, ready to run in case it was a cop...

CHAPTER XXIV

THE MISSIONARY LANDS
ON FOREIGN SHORES

What Keekie Joe beheld caused him to rub his eyes and concentrate his gaze with more intensity than ever he had shown while at his official post. There, bumping against the shore, was somebody or other's grass-plot with a tree on it and a little tent. The frightened natives who had witnessed the arrival of Columbus could not have been more astonished than Keekie Joe.

He glanced out upon the river to see if any lawns or groves or back yards were floating around. Then his gaze returned to the miraculous scene before him. There was the small boy he had known in the morning, "the rich kid" who had been willing to sit as sentinel on the fence.

He was now sitting on an inverted ice cream freezer and all about him on the grass were sandwiches, hundreds of them. The tower had fallen and its ruins lay about Pee-wee's feet. A lantern hung in the tent and through the opening Keekie Joe caught a glimpse of a board covered with spotless white cloth and piled with such things as he had seen in the windows of bakeries. The laden board looked as if a cyclone had struck it but in the tumbled chaos his quick and startled glance could distinguish proud and lofty cakes rolled over on their brown or icy superstructures, and doughnuts looking indeed like the cannon-balls which might have laid low these beauteous edifices.

Keekie Joe gazed upon this scene of mouth-watering ruin with eyes spellbound. Before him lay a miniature Pompeii buried under a kind of lava of whipped cream and custard and chicken salad, amid which toppled cakes and a frowning fortress of gingerbread lay sideways and upside down. Bananas and oranges and nuts and raisins and olives littered the scene of toothsome devastation. An empty square ice cream can, disinterred from its quiet grave of ice, lay upon the ground. Another was in Pee-wee's lap and our hero was armed with a deadly spoon.

"I know who you are," he said, as he annihilated a cocoanut macaroon. "You're the feller I saw this morning. Didn't I tell you if you got to be a scout you'd have all you want to eat? Now you see!"

Keekie Joe did see but he was too astounded to speak. He knew from experience that this strange race of scouts carried jaw-breakers in their pockets, and that they had a deadly aim. But he had not supposed that they travelled in fairy barques which rivalled the windows of bakery shops in their sumptuous appointments. He had not pictured them as travelling on their private islands surrounded by mammoth icing cakes five stories high, and towers of chocolate. He had not fancied them sitting on ice cream freezers and tossing the emptied receptacles from them.

Pee-wee had told his friend of the morning that they would both vote for Keekie Joe and that Keekie Joe should be the patrol leader. If this was the way an ordinary scout travelled, what would be the proper equipment of a patrol leader? It staggered poor Keekie Joe just to think of this. And a scoutmaster!

"Didn't I tell you how it was with scouts?" Pee-wee demanded. "Now you see!"

Keekie Joe rubbed his eyes to make sure he was awake and scrutinized Pee-wee shrewdly. For our hero was somewhat disguised by a villainous moustache of chocolate which reached almost to his ear on one side and made him look like a pirate.

"Do you like sardine sandwiches?" our hero asked at random, for he hardly knew what to use for bait amid such crowding variety. "I was stuck on the flats for over an hour and then the tide took me off. It's coming in now. I'm going to stay on here all night and to-morrow and all next week. So do you want to join? Only you have to be a scout if you want to come on here. There are six other fellers but they're at the party. They said I wouldn't have any fun at the party because I can't dance, but I'm having more fun than any of them. I foiled them. They're all dancing but they're good and hungry. Maybe they look happy but they're not."

"Do dey all go round in dem things?" Keekie Joe ventured to inquire.

"No, but I'm lucky," said Pee-wee.

It seemed to Keekie Joe that Pee-wee was very lucky.

"I've got the best part of the party here," said Pee-wee, holding onto a tree alongshore to keep the island from drifting. "You better hurry up because I can't hold it here;

I can only hold it here about—about—seven seconds. Only you can't come on unless you join because we need one more feller. So will you join? If you will you can have all the ice cream you want, because I got a right to all these things. And there's cake goes with it too, and everything. It includes chicken salad and sandwiches and everything. So will you join? I'm the boss of all these things, I am, you can ask Minerva Skybrow. I'm the boss of the olives and—and—everything."

"Did yer swipe 'em?" Keekie Joe asked, looking furtively around as if he thought that Pee-wee might be shadowed while in possession of such boundless wealth.

"I got them on account of being lucky," Pee-wee said. "I pulled a stick out of the ground and it was a dandy mistake so that shows you'd better stick to me, because I make lots of dandy mistakes. I make them every day; sometimes I make two in one day and I've got nine ideas for next week and all these eats besides. You needn't be afraid to get on," he added, "because it'll drift up the river now and it won't go past Bridgeboro on account of Waring's reef. There's where I want it to stick because if it sticks there it'll stay there, you can bet. Come on, don't you be scared."

Then, with sudden inspiration, he added, "This is a peachy place to lay keekie for cops, because you can see all around you away, *way* off. And when all this food is gone there'll be apples getting ripe on this tree and you won't have to speak for cores either, because you can have whole apples, all you want of them. That's what scouts do, they eat and they stay out all night and they're wild, kind of. And they don't care what happens, and anyway the ice cream is melting all the time, so will you join?"

Keekie Joe, still hesitating in profound astonishment, and a little fearful of this strange apparition with its presiding genius saw that if he were going to act he must act quickly for though Pee-wee was king of the island he seemed not able to govern its capricious fancy. Clutch the tree as he would, the gap between scout and hoodlum persistently widened, and the island seemed bent on hurrying upon its wanton career.

Keekie Joe, not altogether easy in his mind, still found it impossible to resist these enumerated benefits of scouting. Being wild and staying out all night and eating and eating and eating forever and forever under a profusion of blossoms which gave new promise, was too much for the sentinel of Barrel Alley to ignore.

So he ran away to sea as so many other boys had done before him and sailed out upon the briny deep in the good barque Merry-go-round. And he ate such a supper that night as he had never eaten in his life before. Pee-wee had already eaten his fill but he wished to be companionable and make his guest feel at home so he ate another supper with his new friend in accordance with the requirements of good manners.

A scout is polite.

CHAPTER XXV

RETURN OF THE HERO

The lawn party was over, two score or more of famished guests had gone to their homes, the lights in the Skybrow house were out, the sputtering candles in the Japanese lanterns were dying one by one, the grounds were still and dark except for the merry moon which smiled down upon the scene of revelry and tragedy.

At the edge of the lawn where the Isle of Desserts had been, six figures sat in the darkness. They sat in a row, their legs drawn up and held by their clasped hands. They sat waiting and watching in the silent night.

"The river is going to eat the edge of this lawn all away if they don't face it with stone," said Roly Poly.

"Will you please stop talking about eating?" said Brownie.

"I know, but you'd think a rich man like Mr. Skybrow would make provision for a thing like that," said a boy they called Shorty.

"Will you please stop talking about provisions?" said Townsend.

Percy Keese Fitzhugh

"I know, but Nuts was saying—"

"Will you please stop talking about nuts?" said Townsend.

"Well, what shall I talk about then?" Brownie asked.

"Talk about the rhododendron bushes," said Billy. "Look where a big clump was pulled away. Look at that one—all broken. These bushes will have to be all pruned."

"Will you please stop talking about prunes?" said Townsend.

"I know, but seven or eight—"

"Will you please not mention the word ate?" said Townsend. "They ought to be thankful he left the lawn."

"What did his father say over the 'phone?" one asked.

"Oh, he didn't seem to worry," said Townsend. "He knows that the island is on a scow and that the river is small and that his son always lands right side up; that's what he said. I told him the island would come up with the tide and that we'd wait here and row out when he came in sight. He said there was no danger, that the discoverer is always lucky."

"Oh, he's lucky," said Brownie.

"Nothing short of an earthquake can capsize the island," Townsend said.

"He's a whole earthquake in himself," said Billy.

"More than that," said Shorty. "If I owned a restaurant I

wouldn't leave it around, not unless there were buildings on both sides of it."

"And a weight on the top," said Brownie.

"Oh, that goes without saying," said Shorty.

"The blamed thing can't sink, can it?" Billy asked.

"I don't know how heavy his nine ideas are," said Townsend. "They would be the only thing that could sink it."

"We'll reach him easy as pie—"

"Please don't say that word," Townsend pled.

"I think I see the lantern now," said Billy.

"I was afraid he might have eaten that—"

"I could eat it myself," said Roly Poly.

"It's probably all you get," said Townsend.

Pee-wee's surprising coup had not indeed caused any real anxiety in any quarter. It is true that his mother, answering Townsend's thoughtful 'phone call from the Skybrow home, had expressed concern at his being cast up with no companion but a banquet, but no one, not even his parents, feared for his safety.

The river was too tame and narrow, and the island altogether too secure upon its vast scow to introduce the smallest element of peril into his exploit. The tide would have to come up and upon its expanding bosom the gorged hero would return to his native land. Roy and his friends, knowing that Pee-wee's new victims were to rejoin him, went to their several homes to rifle kitchens and turn pantries inside out.

"Yes, that's his light, all right," said Billy.

"That you, Discoverer?" Townsend called, as the light bobbed gayly nearer and nearer. It was coming up the channel.

"Sure," called Pee-wee. "I've got something new! I've got a big surprise for you!"

"Another?" said Townsend.

"It's alive," Pee-wee shouted. "Is the party all over?"

"Oh, absolutely," Townsend called; "you closed it up. Have you got two or three salted almonds over there?"

"Sure," Pee-wee shouted reassuringly, "six or seven."

It was funny with what an air of humorous resignation Townsend Ripley stepped into the skiff and the mock air of ebbing vitality which the others showed was as good as a circus.

"You don't suppose it's some new kind of hunter's stew, do you?" said Townsend resignedly as he languidly took a pair of oars.

"You needn't think I'm coming ashore," called Pee-wee, "because I'm not. Now we've got a full patrol and we're going to live here. There's going to be a boat race next Saturday and I've got two new ideas besides the ones I told you about and I bet I had more fun than you did dancing and somebody's got to go ashore to-morrow and see this feller's mother and father and tell them he's joined the scouts, because he can't go home on account of not having four cigarettes."

Then the boys in the approaching boat could hear Pee-wee saying in a lowered voice to Keekie Joe, "Don't you be scared of them because they won't hurt you."

CHAPTER XXVI

SHORT AND TO THE POINT

Thus began the famous Alligator Patrol, so named because its home was on the water as well as on the land, and also on the mud. Under its flaunting traffic sign many adventures occurred that summer, but the present narrative must be confined to the surprising events which befell during Easter vacation. Later, in the good old summer time, we shall visit the island again if we can find it.

It was a fortunate thing for Keekie Joe that Townsend Ripley was chosen leader of the new patrol. And it was a fortunate thing for everybody that Pee-wee was defeated by a large majority in the election of a camp cook. It is true that every voice was raised for Pee-wee in this stirring campaign when suddenly Townsend turned the traffic sign so it said STOP and that was the end of Pee-wee's chances. "Safety first," said Townsend.

Keekie Joe liked Townsend and felt at home with him. He admired and trusted him because in the beginning Townsend made a point of calling the fellows blokes and guys and talking about "dem t'ings."

"If yez want a guy ter lay keekie, I'll do it fer yez," Keekie Joe said.

"If we see any cops coming," said Townsend, "we'll turn the traffic sign on them and make them stop."

On Sunday morning, Townsend rowed ashore with Keekie Joe and invaded the tenement in Barrel Alley. He took a brand new package of cigarettes to Mr. Keekie Joe, Senior, and Keekie Joe, Junior, was struck dumb with awe at the familiar and persuasive way in which Townsend talked to his parent. The result of the interview was that Keekie Joe returned to the island on a week's furlough from his squalid home. The Barrel Alley gang, which was mobilized in front of Billy Gilson's tire repair shop, made catcalls at the stranger as the pair passed along and when they were some yards distant, several of them summoned Keekie Joe to their loitering conference.

"Hey, Keekie, come 'ere, I want ter tell yer sup'm," one called.

Keekie Joe hesitated and turned. It was a crucial moment in the history of the new patrol.

"Come on back, Keekie," another shouted.

Then it was that Slats Corbett, imperial head of the gang, did a good turn for the scouting movement. He picked up a half dry sponge which was lying in an auto wash pail and hurled it at Townsend Ripley. Without even turning, Townsend raised his hand, caught it, dipped it in the mud at his feet, and walking briskly back, smeared the face and head of the big ungainly bully, leaving him furious and dripping. Keekie Joe trembled at this rash exploit of his new friend and waited in fearful suspense for the sequel.

It was not long in coming. With a roar of obscene invectives, Slats Corbett rushed upon the smiling, slim, quiet stranger, and then in the space of two seconds, there was Slats Corbett lying flat in the mud. In a kind of trance Keekie Joe heard a brisk, pleasant voice.

"Any of the rest of you want any? All right, come along, Joe."

And that really was the ceremony that made Keekie Joe a scout. It is true that they had a kind of formal initiation under the apple tree on Merry-go-round Island and gave him a badge and had him take the oath and so on and so on. And had him hold up his hand—you know how. But it was not when his hand went up that he became a scout. It was when Slats Corbett went down. That was the clincher.

CHAPTER XXVII

SETTLED AT LAST

And now the wandering career of Merry-go-round Island seemed at last to have ended and it roamed no more over the face of the waters. On the contrary, it settled down to a life of respectable retirement on Waring's reef.

Waring's reef was dry land at low tide, and even at high tide was close enough to the surface to support the trusty foundation of the fugitive isle. It stood exactly in the middle of the river at a spot where the stream was straight and comparatively wide, and commanded a fine view of the boat-house a mile or so downstream. There was more or less life down there during the ensuing week for the high school pupils made the place their own in the brief Easter vacation.

It was on Wednesday that a couple of high school boys chugged up in a little launch and were about to land when Pee-wee forbade them by turning the traffic sign upon them just as they were about to set foot on the island. The island had been on its good behavior now for four days and had not so much as turned an inch. It seemed to have found a satisfactory home at last.

Percy Keese Fitzhugh

"What do you call this thing, anyway?" one of the visitors asked.

"It's a desert island," said Pee-wee. "Can't you see what it is? Don't you know a desert island when you see one? Gee whiz, you're in high school, you ought to know a desert island when you see one. I know you," he added, addressing one of the visitors; "you're on the basket-ball team, your name is Chase, your first name is Wingate and you're all the time going around with Grove Bronson's sister and he's in the troop that I'm not in any more."

In the face of these unquestionable facts Wingate Chase was helpless; he could not do otherwise than admit his identity.

"We're going to have some events on Saturday," he said. "This fellow with me is from the Edgemere High School and—"

"He's going to get beaten," shouted Pee-wee; "because Bridgeboro High School can lick all the high schools around here, in athletics and debates and everything."

"That's all right, Kiddo," said the fellow from Edgemere High School.

"You bet it's all right," said Pee-wee.

"We were thinking we'd like to use your island," said Wingate Chase.

"You don't want to take it to Edgemere, do you?" Townsend Ripley asked. "We don't allow it to be taken from the premises. You may use it here if you care to."

"Find out what they want to use it for," shouted Pee-wee.

"What do you want to use it for?" Townsend asked.

"Tell them they'll have to pay for any damage they do to it," Pee-wee said.

"We just want to put a flag on it," Wingate Chase said.

"You mean you want to take possession of it?" Pee-wee demanded. "You mean you want to discover it? *I'm* the discoverer of this desert island."

The fellow from Edgemere seemed rather amused at Pee-wee. "All we want to do," he said, "is to use it to beat the Bridgeboro High School in the rowing match. We just want to row around it. The two crews will start from the boat-house and race upstream and around this island and back. Now that won't hurt the island any, will it? In a few minutes it will be all over except the shouting."

"Shall we let them do it?" Pee-wee whispered to Townsend.

"Of course we'll want one of our referees to stay on the island during the races," said Wingate, "but he won't hurt anything. There'll be several races, a rowing race, a canoe race, a swimming race and so on; we haven't made up the program yet."

"Are you going to have any refreshments?" Pee-wee demanded.

"We don't allow refreshments on the island," said Townsend.

"Shall we let them do it?" Pee-wee asked.

"Positively," said Townsend; "I don't see how we can stop them, as long as they keep outside of the three mile limit. The referee won't do any harm. All he does is to see that the racing is fair as they round the limit."

"We're the limit, hey?" vociferated Pee-wee.

"You said it," laughed the fellow from Edgemere.

"All right," said Pee-wee, "you can do it."

It was not until the Alligator Patrol sat around their camp-fire that night that the possibilities of this participation in the athletic events began to unfold in the seething mind of our hero. He had stood somewhat upon his dignity with the committee because he did not want to hold the island too cheap in their eyes.

Moreover, though he was for Bridgeboro, once, last and always, his attitude was uniformly combative toward older boys, high school boys in particular, and toward high schools generally. He would be chary of the privileges he granted to these "big fellers" whom he knew so well how to "handle." But in the light of the camp-fire he saw visions of huge war profits in these impending combats. While Edgemere and Bridgeboro fought he would become a war millionaire. The little island, retired from its wild career at last and with a secure and fixed abode would still play an important part in world affairs.

"I tell you what we'll do," said Pee-wee; "we'll sell seats for people to see the races from the island. We'll build a couple of benches out of this old refreshment board— we'll drive stakes in the ground—and one of us will go to town—I mean the mainland—with a big sign telling people they can buy seats for ten cents—because in the boat races when Sir Thomas Lipton's yacht got beaten lots of people paid to go out on excursion steamers and this island is better than an excursion steamer, because they'll go right around the edge of it—right around the coast and everybody'll get a dandy view."

Thus it was that on Thursday and Friday there; appeared in the *Bridgeboro Evening Record* an advertisement which read:

> See the High School events on the river from Alligator Island, seats ten cents. Fine view of the races. Free transportation both ways. Alligator Island belongs to the boy scouts and is in the middle of the river, commanding a fine view because the boats go around it. Boat goes back and forth from Gilroy's field. Absolutely safe. Take the beautiful ride to Alligator Island and see the races for only ten cents. Children in arms if not accompanied by parents have to pay five cents.

It will be observed from the advertisement that Merry-go-round Island, alias the Isle of Desserts, was now masquerading under a new name, which had been given it in the hope of obliterating all memories of its wandering past.

Being now a respectable stay-at-home island, stuck fast with each part of its coast true to its proper compass point, what more natural than that its roving youth should be treated as a closed book by its owners? There it sat in the middle of the glinting river, its sturdy understructure reposing upon Waring's reef.

Even at low ride the shallow water rippled about it. At

high tide the coy reef withdrew entirely within the briny deep, so that the unromantic and unsightly scow was not visible and the island stood in all its wild and floral beauty, a vision of picturesque delight for three or four hours each day at full tide. From the mainland (some thirty feet distant according to a piece of string) the yellow dandelions could be seen dotting its geometric coast and occasionally some drowsy turtle, with neck extended, was visible, sleeping in the sun.

The only historic memento of Minerva Skybrow's lawn party to be found upon the island now was the refreshment board, quite empty. It is true that an explorer, delving among the rocks and crevices, might have found some fugitive stuffed olive or perchance a lost nut or raisin here and there. But the feast of Dessert Isle was now a part of history. Minerva's little tent had been delivered to her (for Pee-wee could not eat that) and only the makeshift table which had supported the absconding repast remained.

This was now made into two long benches, supported by sticks driven into the ground. It was intended that the overflow from this grandstand should sit on the grass. These preparations completed, our hero, accompanied by Brownie and Billy, went ashore on Friday afternoon and edified the people on Main Street with an imposing display.

They paraded up and down the sidewalk wearing large placards, the most striking of which was the one that almost completely obscured the diminutive form of our hero. It was appropriately in the form of a sandwich of which he himself was the center, his head and legs protruding from it like the head and legs of a turtle. Its glaring announcement seemed to suggest the literary style of Townsend Ripley.

CUT RATE CRUISES TO ALLIGATOR ISLE

SEE THE WILD SCOUTS AND THE BOAT RACES

ENJOY A SEA VOYAGE IN THE PALATIAL ROWBOAT ALLIGATOR

ROUND AND SQUARE TRIP TEN CENTS.

SAILINGS FROM GILROY'S FIELD.

CHAPTER XXVIII

IT PAYS TO ADVERTISE

On Friday night it rained and the Alligators were driven into their tent. It rained all night and was still raining when the momentous Saturday dawned. They were compelled to eat breakfast in their tent, the top of which was plastered with apple blossoms so that the khaki-colored fabric looked not unlike a brown wall paper with a floral design.

The tide being out, the rain pattered down on the surrounding mud and shallow places, and the members of the patrol sat in the open doorway of their cozy little shelter wistfully gazing at the downpour, and watching the little holes that the raindrops made in the mud.

Each drop, like a bullet, drove a little hole in the oozy bottom, which slowly closed up again. Schools of darting killies hurried this way and that frantically seeking an avenue into the deeper places where puddles would afford them a haven during the lowest ebb. Rain, rain, rain.

On the porch of the boat-house a mile or so down-stream was gathered a group of young fellows, also watching wistfully. Through the intervening space of rain they seemed like pictures of spectres, misty and unsubstantial.

"The lowest ebb is the turn of the tide," said Townsend cheerily. "I think when it comes in it's going to stop raining, that's what I think. It's going to clear up and be warm this afternoon, you see. Rain before seven, clear before eleven. What do you say we catch some of those killies and fry them?"

"That's what you call an inspiration," said Roly Poly.

They caught some killies with a bent pin and fried them and they were not half bad.

Along about eleven o'clock the tide began running up, the killies which had not been lured to their undoing, disappeared in the swelling water, and soon the ripples danced up over the mud, submerging it entirely. The river began to be attractive again. And then the sun came out.

"This is going to be some peach of a tide for races," said Townsend; "it will be good and full after such an all night rain."

At two o'clock, when the river was about half full, a launch came chugging up from the boat club bringing a flag and the young fellow who was to be posted at the turning point. He planted the flag on its tall standard near the shore and settled down to mind his own business. Pee-wee received him as if he were a foreign ambassador.

Our hero was now so intent upon his commercial enterprise that he forgot all about the races except in their commercial aspect. The island was but the turning point for the contestants and seemed detached from the excitement and preparations which prevailed down at the club house.

Soon, along the shore, there began to be visible little groups of boys sprawling on the grass, waiting. The boathouse porch and the adjacent float were filled with high school pupils. They made a great racket, and from all the noise and bustle thereabouts the little island seemed removed, as if a part of the events and yet not a part.

Presently a little group of girls appeared at the edge of Gilroy's Field, which was the nearest point on the mainland to Alligator Island. They seemed to be looking about in a bewildered, inquiring sort of way. Evidently the advertising was bringing results. It seemed as if they might have banded together (as girls will) for the cut rate cruise which they had seen advertised. At all events they seemed to be strangers. Whoever they were, it spoke well for their adventurous spirit that they should wish to book passage to an unknown shore, when there were no others in sight who seemed the least interested in the voyage.

"Is that Alligator Island?" one of them called.

"It certainly is," Townsend answered. "I'll come over and get you; the boat is leaving right away."

"Have your fares ready," Pee-wee called in a voice of thunder.

As Townsend approached the mainland there was much whispering and giggling among the girls. "We came from Edgemere," said one of them; "we're in the Edgemere High School and we came over on the trolley to see the Bridgeboro High School beaten. We saw a small boy in the street with a sign—"

"That was me," shouted Pee-wee; "I saw you on Main Street. Have your fares ready and he'll bring you over. All aboard! All aboard to Alligator Island with its tropic vegetarians and boat races!" And, in his excitement and enthusiasm he added, "Step this way! Step right this way!"

"Did you ever hear of such a thing," laughed one girl.

"He means after you step out of the boat," said Townsend.

You would have thought that Pee-wee was selling desert islands out of a basket. He stood on the extreme edge nearest to the field, shouting, "Here you are, this way for your desert isle! See the tropic variations—"

"He means vegetation," said Townsend.

"He means fresh vegetables," called Brownie.

"Here you are for your fresh vegetables," Pee-wee shouted, hardly knowing what he said at this actual prospect of business which he saw before his very eyes. "The races encircle this island. Here you are for your best seats! Come early and avoid the rush!"

"That's the wild man of the island," Townsend said; "he's perfectly harmless: step right in the boat."

They were rowed over and escorted to seats, where they did not have to wait long, for scarcely were they settled on one long bench when a chorus of shouts arose down at the boat-house, as out into the river shot two canoes.

"Oh, they're coming! They're *coming*!" the girls carolled in great excitement and anticipation.

"Oh, look! Do *look*!" one of them said, clutching the shoulder of her neighbor. "He's in the red canoe! It's Willie Dawdle, and he's ahead! *Hurrah for Edgemere*! Oh, he's *coming*, he's *coming*! I knew we'd *annihilate* them, I just *knew* it! Oh, it's simply *glorious*!"

"Hurrah for Bridgeboro!" shouted Pee-wee.

"Hurrah for Edgemere!" shouted the girls.

The two canoes, with Edgemere a little ahead as well as they could see, came gliding up the river, two streaks, red and green, in the sunshine…

CHAPTER XXIX

THE RACE

The canoe race, which was the first of the events, was also the best—as well as the last. Never was there wilder excitement on Pee-wee's island than when the green and red canoes glided northward, approaching the turning point.

The red canoe skilfully paddled by the Edgemere champion, Willie Dawdle, was some ahead and gaining rapidly and the girls from Edgemere High School could not contain themselves for joy. Among the Alligator Patrol, too, the excitement ran high and shout upon shout for Bridgeboro arose as Wingate Chase spurted to get the inner turn about the island. He gained fast now and as the distance between the two canoes shortened the air was rent with deafening yells for Bridgeboro.

The two contestants were abreast when suddenly amid the uproar could be heard a voice, a voice singularly matter-of-fact and sensible, uttering words which if not of excitement seemed at least pertinent to the occasion, "How are they going to go around that blamed thing when it's sailing up the river?"

Alas, it was too true. The most unusual development which could possibly complicate an athletic event had occurred; the turning point had deserted the race and was sailing majestically up the river. It had already sailed a hundred feet or so before the watchers on the mainland discovered the fact.

As for the striving contestants they were too intent upon the race to perceive the strange turn of affairs until the wild mirth upon the "mainland" apprised them of it. They must have looked funny enough from the shore frantically pursuing the fugitive turning post, and the unhallowed joy of the spectators was only increased by Pee-wee's heroic efforts in the emergency as with a long pole he strove to stay the progress of the recreant island. Failing in these herculean efforts, he still tried to save the day by shouting to the racers.

"*Keep up! Keep up!*" he yelled. "You can go around it. You're going faster than the island is. *Don't give up!* It makes it all the more exciting. It's like—like—like—kind of—like running up an escalator! Don't stop! Keep it up, it's an escalator race!"

It certainly made it "all the more exciting." As for the inhabitants of the island, they were carried away in more than one sense. Townsend lay flat upon the ground in a spasm of silent laughter. Several others of the new Alligator Patrol sat on the edge of the stern and rock-bound coast, their legs dangling in the water, and seemed in danger of falling in, so gymnastic was their merriment. As for the occupants or the grandstand, they probably thought (if they were able to think at all) that ten cents was a small price to pay for such an exciting race.

Only one occupant of the fleeing island was up and about

and fully conscious. With his companions lying flat or doubled up and screaming so that the woods along shore echoed with their insane mirth, our hero stood amid the chaos, shouting to the racers at the top of his voice. They were almost abreast of him now, and laughing themselves, for the race had become a farce.

"Come on! Keep it up!" he shouted. "You can go around it while it's sailing just as good as if it were standing still! The race kind of stretches out like an elastic—it's an extensible race. Keep it up! Keep it up!"

"Don't," moaned Townsend from his place on the ground. "This is too much—"

"It isn't enough!" Pee-wee shouted. "The race is better because it's longer—it stretches out—it's an extensible race—I invented it—"

"What on earth is the cause of it?" laughed one of the girls.

"Extra—extra—ex—ex—ex—extra high tide caused by the r—r—rain," shrieked Townsend, hardly able to get the words out. "This is the cli—cli—climax of Eas—Eas—Easter vac—c—c—c—c—*cation*!"

Amid screams and catcalls from the shore an official launch came chugging up the course. By that time the two canoeists had given themselves up to laughter and sat shaking as their canoes drifted. Only the island continued merrily upon the flood tide.

"Called off?" somebody called from the shore.

"Certainly it's called off," said the official in the launch.

"This was supposed to be a race, not a game of tag."

"*Come on! Come on!*" screamed Pee-wee from the departing isle. "Hurrah for Bridgeboro High! Come on, you can go around us! If a man can—listen, I've got a dandy argument—if a man can shoot a bird on the wing a race like that is just as good—you can encircle an island on the wing too! *Come on! Come on!* It's a new kind of a race! A lot of girls paid ten cents to see it! Come on, go around us!"

"Oh, *gracious, goodness*, we've had our money's worth," moaned one of the girls; "we're not complaining."

"It's like a movie play," screamed another.

"It's a very move—m—moving drama," stammered Townsend.

"And all for ten cents," said one of the girls.

"They're not coming!" Pee-wee shouted. "We won the race! We weren't in it but we won it anyway. That feller in the launch is crazy! It was a chase and a race all in one—it was a chase race—I invented it and he went and spoiled it all."

Time and tide wait for no man. Up the swelling river, out of the voice range of the hooting throng, farther and still farther from the madding crowd, sailed Turning Post Island, alias Merry-go-round Island, alias Isle of Desserts, alias Alligator Isle, alias The Earthly Paradise.

Other motor-boats, manned by astonished officials and bearing committees, chugged up to where the island had been and a flotilla of rowboats and canoes hovered thereabouts while their occupants inspected curiously the place where the official turning point with its crowded grandstand had been. But the official turning point had vanished, though the voice of our hero could still be beard up beyond Collison's bend.

And still Townsend Ripley lay prone and laughed and laughed and laughed.

"Your money will be refunded, of course," he managed to say to the several occupants of the grandstand. "You see we had a heavy rain all night and—"

"Oh, don't *speak* of returning our money," one of the girls laughed. "We really ought to pay you *more*."

"We can't take any more," Pee-wee shouted. "You—you get the ride for nothing—it's thrown in—because I said free transportation and a scout has to keep his word. Even if we float miles and miles we can't take another cent—"

"We may be rovers but we're not profiteers," moaned Townsend.

"If—if we don't drift to shore by supper time," said Pee-wee, "you get your dinner too just like when an ocean steamer is delayed in a fog; they give you your dinner, so don't you worry because you're with scouts and when it gets to be six o'clock I'll make a hunter's stew."

At this there was a sudden noise as of horror and anguish and before our voyagers realized what was happening, Townsend Ripley had rolled off the island into the water.

CHAPTER XXX

ABSENCE MAKES THE ISLAND QUIET

"It's all right," Townsend sputtered as he crawled ashore. "I was just thinking of something sad; I feel better now. It was one of the finest races that I never saw."

"It would have been a good race," said Pee-wee with a frown indicative of withering scorn, "only they had to go and break it up. *Just because we moved*—do you call that an argument? *We* ought to get the silver cup, that's what *I* think. They could have—have—headed us off, couldn't they? The rule said they had to go around this flag, it didn't say anything about where the flag would be. That's a teckinality. Anyway, I'm glad we're rid of them."

"We seem to be making port," said Townsend. "I don't know just where we are. I think if we were to cut up through these woods—You girls want to get to the Edgemere trolley, I suppose?"

"That's the idea," said one of them.

"Well, then, let's see," Townsend ruminated.

"I'll take you to the trolley," Pee-wee shouted, as the

island gave evidence of an intention to bunk into the east bank of the river. "Because I know how to find my way in the woods—scouts have to know all those things—I can tell by moss and hop-toads and things, which is east and west. I'll take you to the trolley. If we should get lost in the woods I know how to cook bark so you can eat it, only scouts don't get lost. So do you want me to take you to the trolley?"

Brownie was about to whisper his disapproval of this to Townsend but Townsend cut him short. "Let him do it," he said; "if he stays here he'll make a hunter's stew. We can put one over on him by cooking supper while he's gone. Safety first. If he goes ashore they may get lost, if he stays here we're *all* lost."

"True," said Billy.

"Absolutely correct," said Brownie.

"That's what you call an argument," said Roly Poly.

"It's a teckinality," said Nuts.

"Discoverer," said Townsend, "the patrol thinks that you are the proper one to escort our guests to the Edgemere trolley."

"Isn't that perfectly *lovely*!" said one of the girls.

"If the woods should wander away while you're in them," said Townsend, "send up a smoke signal and we'll come and rescue you. Don't hurry back, Discoverer; remember, these girls come first of all. We'll tie the island to a tree and have a game of mumbly peg. You'll find us here when you get back."

"Well," said Townsend, after he had securely fastened the island to shore by a piece of rope, "let's make hay while the sun shines and get supper. In an hour or so it may be too late. After all our adventures I feel that another hunter's stew—"

"If the island saw another hunter's stew it would run away," said Brownie.

"We've had quite a week of it, hey?" said Billy.

"Yes, I don't think I've ever been around so much in a week before," said Townsend; "I feel like a pinwheel."

"Or a top," said Brownie.

"Something like that," said Townsend. "Well, Joe, what do you think of us?" he added, sprawling on the ground as was his wont. The others began preparations for supper.

"How about some spaghetti?" Roly Poly asked. "Could you eat some spaghetti?"

"I might if I were coaxed," said Townsend. "How about you, Joe?"

Townsend had made it his religious duty all through that week to consult Keekie Joe about every meal, and indeed about everything that was to be done. He jealously saw to it that Joe had a voice in everything. Not that any of them denied Joe these rights, but Joe felt out of place among these strange boys and the boys sometimes forgot about him.

It was exactly like Pee-wee to drag poor Joe head over heels into scouting, and then forget all about him. It was exactly like Townsend Ripley to take the poor little hoodlum quietly in hand and be his friend and sponsor. He treated him always as an equal and as a comrade. What the others forgot, he remembered.

He agreed with Joe, or disagreed with him, as pals will agree and disagree. He always took him seriously. He allowed Joe to teach him to play craps and then said he didn't see much fun in it, and such was his magnetic power over poor Joe that Joe said he didn't see any fun in it either. And there was an end of it.

So it was with all the wretched hoodlum games and tricks that poor Joe had known; one by one they failed in the test, and he became ashamed of them. It is no wonder that Keekie Joe worshipped this keen, easy-going patrol leader, who seemed to be no leader at all. Even Pee-wee was sacrificed in the good cause and Townsend made fun of Pee-wee for Keekie Joe's amusement.

As they sprawled about the fire that Saturday night, the last night but one of their outlandish vacation, and ate spaghetti from tin platters, the trend of the talk showed somewhat the effects of the week's outing upon the poor little derelict of Barrel Alley.

"Seems good sitting here and not eating hunter's stew, doesn't it?" said Townsend in his funny way. "I never realized how much I enjoyed not eating hunter's stew. I shall always love hunter's stew for the pleasure it has given me when I didn't eat it. I suppose the Discoverer ought to be getting back pretty soon."

"Unless those girls took him to Edgemere," said Brownie.

"I don't think they'd do that, they spoke well of

Edgemere," said Townsend.

"There's no telling where he'll drift to," said Nuts.

"Please don't talk about drifting," said Townsend. "The way I feel about drifting I don't ever want to look at a snow-drift. I can't even listen to the drift of a person's conversation. How about *you*, Joe?"

"De Discov'r's all right," said Joe, loyally.

"I wouldn't say he's all right," said Townsend; "but when he's wrong he's at his best. That's what *I* think, Joe."

"He's always at his best," said Brownie.

"Except when he's at his worst," said Townsend, "and then he's best of all. That's logic, as he would say. I wonder what he'll bring back with him. Let's each guess; I guess a carpet sweeper. How about *you*, Joe?"

Joe only smiled, but did not venture a guess.

"I guess an alarm clock and a headlight from an automobile," said Brownie.

"I guess part of a floor lamp—the shade part," said Billy.

"I guess—I guess," said Nuts; "let's see—I guess some chicken wire, part of a typewriter machine and a megaphone."

"You're all wrong and I'm right as you usually are," said Townsend; "he will bring back—"

"Let's go in swimming," said Brownie.

"Good idea," said Townsend. "Joe, I'm going to teach you to swim."

Now it was right then that Keekie Joe said something which surprised them all. And it was just that little remark which showed the effects of the week's outing upon his simple mind. He had certainly not received any particular training or instruction; he had been in some measure a participant but mostly a bashful and amused witness of his companions' adventures and a silent listener to their talk.

He had heard them all speak of their parents and of how this or that plan might be approved or disapproved at home. He had heard them discuss whether their parents would probably expect them home on Sunday night or early Monday morning. Perhaps it was not a sense of dutiful obedience, but rather a certain budding pride in the bosom of Keekie Joe, which caused him to make the remark which surprised them.

He would let them know that he too had a parent, though no one had thought to speak of his parents. If he could not have clothes like them at least he could have obligations like them. Perhaps the true spirit of obedience was not in him. But the point is that the poor little wretch had discovered a certain pride within himself and wished to boast of a restraint which a week previously he would have ignored. He too had someone who was interested in his goings and comings. So he said,

"Me mudder sez I dasn' go swimmin' widout she leaves me."

It was strange how Keekie Joe, who had disregarded his poor mother's wishes on so many occasions, should present her now to his new friends. He did not have any of the things which they had, bicycles, tents, cooking sets, radio sets; but one thing he had as well as they, a mother. And so he used her as they used theirs. He played her as his only card.

"Me mudder sez I dasn' go swimmin' widout she leaves me."

"Good for you, Joe," said Townsend, "I'll see your mother next week and fix it. *And you do just what she told you to do till then.* You've got the right idea, Joe." And he hit Joe a good rap on the shoulder in his friendly way...

CHAPTER XXXI

A PROMISE

When he had put the racing fans on the Edgemere trolley, Pee-wee, like Jack ashore, betook himself into Bridgeboro to have his fling before returning to the ship. The habit of sailors home from long voyages is well known, and we need not be surprised to find him bending his steps toward Bennett's Fresh Confectionery, where he climbed onto one of the stools before the soda fountain.

He had just consumed a raspberry ice cream soda and was considering the question of whether he should have another when he noticed somebody which reminded him of the doom which awaited him on Monday morning. This was Miss Carlton who taught in the Bridgeboro Public School. She had just consummated the purchase of a box of candy and such were the cordial relations between herself and Pee-wee (out of school) that she proffered him the box for a choice of its contents.

"I don't know whether to take a chocolate one or a white one," Pee-wee said.

"Why not take both?" she suggested.

"I guess maybe that would be safest, hey?" he said.

"And what have you been doing all week?" Miss Carlton asked.

"I've been at sea," Pee-wee said; "I've been floating around on a desert island that's on a scow and this is the first day I came ashore. I started a new patrol and Keekie Joe is in it. He's in your class, isn't he?"

"He is—sometimes," said Miss Carlton ruefully.

"He goes on the hook a lot, doesn't he?" said Pee-wee.

"Oh, lots and lots," said Miss Carlton; dubiously.

"But anyway, don't you care," said Pee-wee, "because now he's a scout and he'll go to school every day, because a scout's honor has to be trusted. Do you know what was in that white one? Kind of lemon like."

"Won't you have another?"

"Brown and white are our patrol colors," said Pee-wee. "We just started our new patrol."

"Take a brown one and a white one," said Miss Carlton.

"I bet you don't know the name of our new patrol. It's the Alligators."

"I think that's a good name for Joe McKinny," said Miss Carlton; "he's so slow coming to school."

"I can prove you're wrong about him," said Pee-wee, "because alligators don't go to school and—"

"Won't you have another, Walter?"

"One for good measure, hey?" said Pee-wee. "Anyway, how much do you want to bet he won't go to school now? Because he will, because scouts have to do what they're supposed to do and I bet you he'll—"

"Another, Walter?"

"I'll take a pink one this time. I bet you he'll go to school and be all right on account of starting to be a scout. I got some money for grandstand seats on our island to see the boat races and I'll treat you to a soda."

"Thank you," laughed Miss Carlton, "but I think not now."

Miss Carlton knew Pee-wee well enough (for he had been in her class) not to inquire particularly about his multifarious adventures. She knew that they were too numerous and complicated for casual recital. Nor had she any faith in the influence of scouting on Keekie Joe. She did not believe that any power in the world could tempt Keekie Joe to school on a Monday, because Keekie Joe's partiality to liberal week ends was well known to her.

"Well, I only hope it will do him some good,"; said Miss Carlton dubiously.

"You mean scouting? *Sure* it will. You just wait and see. So long, maybe I'll see you on Monday."

"Won't you have one more?" the tempter urged.

Pee-wee hesitated. "I'll take a cocoanut one," he said, "because they're small. So long, I'll see you later."

Thus it was that when Pee-wee went back to the island, he did take something with him which was not named in the guessing of his friends. It was the heavy responsibility which he bore to make scouting good in the eyes of Miss Carlton. His promise, made at the altar of Bennett's candy counter and solemnized by a dozen assorted dainties, must be fulfilled.

He found his friends sprawling around their dying campfire on the island. Townsend was lying on his back as usual, his hands clasped behind his head, his eyes fixed on the quiet stars. Crowds thronged the main street of Bridgeboro on that Saturday night but the island lay peacefully against the shore of the wood skirting the river and the town might have been a hundred miles on for all the campers could tell.

"Well, we've had quite a week," said Townsend; "and now that we're started I hope we'll stick together and make a real, honest-to-goodness patrol. Joe is with us to the last ditch—out for the second rate badge—"

"You mean the second *class* badge," Pee-wee thundered.

"Brownie is going to be steward or whatever you—"

"Don't talk about stew," said Billy.

"Pardon me, my fault," said Townsend, "only I'd like to rise to remark while I'm lying here that I think we're going to make a pretty nifty patrol. Joe wouldn't go in swimming on account of his mother; couldn't force him to it, so there you are."

"And he's going to school Monday," said Pee-wee; "because I met his teacher in the—the—eh—the store."

"Candy store?"

"How did you know?" Pee-wee gasped.

"Just an inspiration," said Townsend.

"And I told her he's going to school every single day after this," said Pee-wee. "So are you?" he demanded of Keekie Joe.

"Posilutely he is, if not more so," said Townsend. "Every day except Saturday. He's even willing to eat hunter's stew and a fellow that will do that doesn't mind school; he can stand anything. How about that, Joe?"

"I gotta do what you sez," said Joe.

"There you are," said Townsend. "What more do you want? We're *all* going to school because the school won't come to us. So now let's tell riddles till we get tired of hearing each other talk and then we'll turn in. And we'll camp here all day to-morrow and to-morrow night, and the next day-school."

"I know a riddle," shouted Pee-wee. "Why is a stu—"

"Stop!" shouted Townsend.

"I was going to ask a riddle about a stu—"

A chorus of protest drowned his voice.

"A stu—" he roared, "debaker. It's a riddle about a Stude-baker car!"

"Let's tell Ford stories!" shouted Brownie.

"I know a lot of them!" shouted Pee-wee.

"Why is this island like a Ford car?" Townsend asked.

"Why?"

"What's the answer?"

"Because there are a lot of nuts on it," said Townsend. "Why is Scout Harris like a Ford? Because he's small but makes a lot of noise. Horrible! Here's a better one. Why is—"

"I know one! I know one!" shouted Pee-wee.

"Let's see if we can catch some eels," said Townsend.

CHAPTER XXXII

VENGEANCE

On Sunday night they turned in for their last sleep on the island. That the island had proved a quitter on two momentous occasions had not prejudiced them against it. With all its faults they loved it still. The only thing they had against it was that it would not remain still.

Though it was small and of an unromantic squareness, it seemed the center of a vast empire during the week which was now ending and they were sorry at the thought of leaving it. But at least the Alligator Patrol was started and, like the island itself, nothing could stop it.

The night was chilly so they slept in the tent. So profound was their sleep that they did not hear the dipping oars of an approaching boat which came down the river after midnight. This boat was dilapidated and leaky but it was a vision of beauty compared to its occupants. These were none other than Slats Corbett, imperial head of Barrel Alley, and his official staff, consisting of Skinny Mattenburg and Spider McCurren. Such nocturnal excursions were not uncommon with them.

Nor were they surprised to see the new habitat of their

official sentinel bobbing against the wooded shore. Indeed, some tidings of Joe's adventurous career (since he had run away to sea) had penetrated to Barrel Alley and the only thing which had prevented the alleyites from making an assault upon the island was the presence there of Townsend Ripley. Him they had come to regard with a kind of superstitious awe because he was so precipitate and decisive.

The fact that he had allowed no time for preliminary threats and profanity, rather baffled these hoodlums. He had a quaint way of cutting out all the customary boasts and menaces preceding an encounter, and going straight to the heart of the matter.

Therefore, Slats Corbett did not undertake anything in the way of a belligerent and retaliatory enterprise now. But he could not pass the sleeping campers without in some way registering his mortal enmity, so he did something which was altogether characteristic of him. He rowed very quietly along shore and untied the rope with which the little island was moored. Even this unheroic thing he did in fear and trembling, for the spirit of Townsend Ripley seemed to pervade the quiet spot. Then the trio proceeded quietly down the river in the darkness.

CHAPTER XXXIII

KEEKIE JOE, SCOUT

The first one to awake in the morning was Keekie Joe. Going to school on Monday was such an unusual thing with him that he had awakened at five o'clock, and had not been able to go to sleep again. He had a strange, nervous feeling as if he might be going to his own wedding.

The school would look strange on a Monday. Ordinarily after a week's vacation he would have taken both Monday and Tuesday. But now, strange to say, he wanted to go to school. He wanted to do what the rest of them did. Oh, no, he was not a new boy all made over, he was just poor little Keekie Joe, but he was going to do what the rest of them did that day…

He now discovered, to his surprise, that the island was in the middle of the river. It had, in fact, started drifting downstream on the ebbing tide, and had caught again on Waring's reef, the scene of its recent exploit. It would stick there for some hours now, at least, for the tide was running out.

Keekie Joe looked all about him, then stole cautiously to

Percy Keese Fitzhugh

the tent and looked within. His friends were sleeping soundly. He withdrew from the tent and looked about again. The island was about a mile farther downstream than where it had been moored.

Looking down the river, Keekie Joe could see the boathouse, and the gilt ball on top of the flagpole shone dazzling in the early sunlight. The shores and river seemed fresh and new and clean, bathed in the growing light of the new day.

For a minute it seemed to Keekie Joe as if he were a sentinel again, "layin' keekie" while his friends slept. In the trees along shore the birds were already chirping, a merry fish (that did not have to go to school) flopped out of the water and went splashing into the dim coolness again, from very excess of joy, as it seemed. Perhaps he had just looked out to see what kind of a day it was going to be. In the field on the farther shore from town stood several cows, like statues of contentment.

Suddenly, Keekie Joe remembered that Pee-wee's palatial cruising boat *Alligator* had been drawn, not up on the shore of the island but up on the shore nearby. Therefore, it was not at the island now. It was a mile upstream, drawn up under a willow tree at the edge of the woods. Keekie Joe scanned the shore as far as he could see, but he could not discover any sign of it. However, he knew where it was.

He wondered how his friends and he would get to shore to go to school. He knew they could swim, but they would get their clothes soaked and could not go to school in such condition. Poor Keekie Joe! It never occurred to him that some boys have two suits of clothes, and that his dripping friends might go home and change their clothes before going to school.

Keekie Joe knew (or at least thought) that this situation would become serious when school time neared. He was anxious to know what time it was. You see, Joe was not a regular full-fledged scout and he could not tell time by the sun nor by forty-eleven other ingenious means known to Scout Harris.

His whole standing capital now was a knowledge of how to swim, and a dawning consciousness that scouting meant helping people and all that sort of thing. Thanks to a long course of disobedience to his poor mother, he had learned to swim like a water rat. He had had somewhat the advantage of other boys in this respect for he had gone swimming Mondays when they were in school.

But he could not determine even approximately what time it was and he had no watch. He knew that it was early, but he also knew that a mile was a long distance, especially against the tide.

Then it occurred to him that he might steal ever so cautiously into the tent and carefully, *ever so carefully*, pull Townsend's watch out from under his rough pillow and find out just what time it was. Keekie Joe had heard some wonderful stories about stalking; from all accounts rendered by Pee-wee that scout of scouts had hoodwinked every creature in the animal kingdom, stealing up behind them unawares, and subjecting every variety of bird to nervous prostration.

But Keekie Joe decided not to try his skill at this kind of stalking. For one thing, he had never touched a gold watch before and the thought of it awed him. And for another thing, if Townsend should awake and catch him in the act he would think that his protege was trying to steal his watch...

CHAPTER XXXIV

THE STORY CLOSES AND SCHOOL OPENS

Keekie Joe could not trust himself in any such stalking exploit and he had no standing capital of good reputation with which to verify his honorable intention in case his bungling hand should slip. He had as good as promised Townsend that he would not go swimming. But also these boys all had to go to school.

I am not saying what I think he should have done; I am simply telling you what he did. He slid silently into the water with his rags clinging to him and started swimming up the river against the ebbing tide. He had a simple, short-sighted, one-track mind. It never occurred to him that by undressing he might return and don his dry clothes again, such as they were. He had always gone in swimming with his rags on and he was his own clothesline; they dried upon his back.

In the water, Keekie Joe was at his best. He swam to shore like a little devil. Then, with all his might and main, he ran northward through the woods keeping close to the shore. This necessitated his swimming through mud and marshy places. But he hurried on, soaked, weary, panting. He was a horrible sight when he reached the boat, dripping with mud, his flesh torn by brambles, his ragged clothing plastered to his poor little form like wall-paper.

He was not good at rowing but fortunately all he had to do was to guide the old punt while the tide carried it down. And so he brought the old boat to the island and pulled it well up on the shore, and tied it with a rope. Then panting, dripping, he groped his way to the tent and looked within. They were all still sleeping peacefully.

Keekie Joe had no change of clothing either on the island or anywhere else. Going to school was out of the question now; he was too saturated and filthy. Why should he remain on the island? He felt that he could not face Townsend Ripley after breaking the promise he had made him not to go in swimming. Poor Keekie Joe, his eyes were so full of mud that he could not see the glory of that broken promise!

"Yez cin all go ter school," he said. Then, with as much fear and stealth as if he were running away from the police he crept into the water again and started for shore. He bent his course as nearly as he could for the end of Barrel Alley which abutted on the river. Soon he would be back in the yard of Billy Gilson's tire repair shop and could rest. His little sojourn in Fairyland had been a wonderful thing…

Other books by this author

Tom Slade at Black Lake

Tom Slade's Double Dare

Tom Slade with the Boys Over There

Tom Slade with the Colors

Tom Slade Motorcycle Dispatch Bearer

Tom Slade Mystery Trail

Tom Slade at Temple Camp

Pee-Wee Harris on the Trail

Roy Blakeley

Roy Blakeley's Adventures in Camp

Percy Keese Fitzhugh

Choose from Thousands of 1stWorldLibrary Classics By

A. M. Barnard
Ada Leverson
Adolphus William Ward
Aesop
Agatha Christie
Alexander Aaronsohn
Alexander Kielland
Alexandre Dumas
Alfred Gatty
Alfred Ollivant
Alice Duer Miller
Alice Turner Curtis
Alice Dunbar
Allen Chapman
Alleyne Ireland
Ambrose Bierce
Amelia E. Barr
Amory H. Bradford
Andrew Lang
Andrew McFarland Davis
Andy Adams
Angela Brazil
Anna Alice Chapin
Anna Sewell
Annie Besant
Annie Hamilton Donnell
Annie Payson Call
Annie Roe Carr
Annonaymous
Anton Chekhov
Archibald Lee Fletcher
Arnold Bennett
Arthur C. Benson
Arthur Conan Doyle
Arthur M. Winfield
Arthur Ransome
Arthur Schnitzler
Arthur Train
Atticus
B.H. Baden-Powell
B. M. Bower
B. C. Chatterjee
Baroness Emmuska Orczy
Baroness Orczy
Basil King
Bayard Taylor
Ben Macomber
Bertha Muzzy Bower
Bjornstjerne Bjornson

Booth Tarkington
Boyd Cable
Bram Stoker
C. Collodi
C. E. Orr
C. M. Ingleby
Carolyn Wells
Catherine Parr Traill
Charles A. Eastman
Charles Amory Beach
Charles Dickens
Charles Dudley Warner
Charles Farrar Browne
Charles Ives
Charles Kingsley
Charles Klein
Charles Hanson Towne
Charles Lathrop Pack
Charles Romyn Dake
Charles Whibley
Charles Willing Beale
Charlotte M. Braeme
Charlotte M. Yonge
Charlotte Perkins Stetson
Clair W. Hayes
Clarence Day Jr.
Clarence E. Mulford
Clemence Housman
Confucius
Coningsby Dawson
Cornelis DeWitt Wilcox
Cyril Burleigh
D. H. Lawrence
Daniel Defoe
David Garnett
Dinah Craik
Don Carlos Janes
Donald Keyhoe
Dorothy Kilner
Dougan Clark
Douglas Fairbanks
E. Nesbit
E. P. Roe
E. Phillips Oppenheim
E. S. Brooks
Earl Barnes
Edgar Rice Burroughs
Edith Van Dyne
Edith Wharton

Edward Everett Hale
Edward J. O'Biren
Edward S. Ellis
Edwin L. Arnold
Eleanor Atkins
Eleanor Hallowell Abbott
Eliot Gregory
Elizabeth Gaskell
Elizabeth McCracken
Elizabeth Von Arnim
Ellem Key
Emerson Hough
Emilie F. Carlen
Emily Bronte
Emily Dickinson
Enid Bagnold
Enilor Macartney Lane
Erasmus W. Jones
Ernie Howard Pie
Ethel May Dell
Ethel Turner
Ethel Watts Mumford
Eugene Sue
Eugenie Foa
Eugene Wood
Eustace Hale Ball
Evelyn Everett-green
Everard Cotes
F. H. Cheley
F. J. Cross
F. Marion Crawford
Fannie E. Newberry
Federick Austin Ogg
Ferdinand Ossendowski
Fergus Hume
Florence A. Kilpatrick
Fremont B. Deering
Francis Bacon
Francis Darwin
Frances Hodgson Burnett
Frances Parkinson Keyes
Frank Gee Patchin
Frank Harris
Frank Jewett Mather
Frank L. Packard
Frank V. Webster
Frederic Stewart Isham
Frederick Trevor Hill
Frederick Winslow Taylor

Friedrich Kerst
Friedrich Nietzsche
Fyodor Dostoyevsky
G.A. Henty
G.K. Chesterton
Gabrielle E. Jackson
Garrett P. Serviss
Gaston Leroux
George A. Warren
George Ade
Geroge Bernard Shaw
George Cary Eggleston
George Durston
George Ebers
George Eliot
George Gissing
George MacDonald
George Meredith
George Orwell
George Sylvester Viereck
George Tucker
George W. Cable
George Wharton James
Gertrude Atherton
Gordon Casserly
Grace E. King
Grace Gallatin
Grace Greenwood
Grant Allen
Guillermo A. Sherwell
Gulielma Zollinger
Gustav Flaubert
H. A. Cody
H. B. Irving
H. C. Bailey
H. G. Wells
H. H. Munro
H. Irving Hancock
H. R. Naylor
H. Rider Haggard
H. W. C. Davis
Haldeman Julius
Hall Caine
Hamilton Wright Mabie
Hans Christian Andersen
Harold Avery
Harold McGrath
Harriet Beecher Stowe
Harry Castlemon
Harry Coghill
Harry Houidini

Hayden Carruth
Helent Hunt Jackson
Helen Nicolay
Hendrik Conscience
Hendy David Thoreau
Henri Barbusse
Henrik Ibsen
Henry Adams
Henry Ford
Henry Frost
Henry James
Henry Jones Ford
Henry Seton Merriman
Henry W Longfellow
Herbert A. Giles
Herbert Carter
Herbert N. Casson
Herman Hesse
Hildegard G. Frey
Homer
Honore De Balzac
Horace B. Day
Horace Walpole
Horatio Alger Jr.
Howard Pyle
Howard R. Garis
Hugh Lofting
Hugh Walpole
Humphry Ward
Ian Maclaren
Inez Haynes Gillmore
Irving Bacheller
Isabel Cecilia Williams
Isabel Hornibrook
Israel Abrahams
Ivan Turgenev
J. G.Austin
J. Henri Fabre
J. M. Barrie
J. M. Walsh
J. Macdonald Oxley
J. R. Miller
J. S. Fletcher
J. S. Knowles
J. Storer Clouston
J. W. Duffield
Jack London
Jacob Abbott
James Allen
James Andrews
James Baldwin

James Branch Cabell
James DeMille
James Joyce
James Lane Allen
James Lane Allen
James Oliver Curwood
James Oppenheim
James Otis
James R. Driscoll
Jane Abbott
Jane Austen
Jane L. Stewart
Janet Aldridge
Jens Peter Jacobsen
Jerome K. Jerome
Jessie Graham Flower
John Buchan
John Burroughs
John Cournos
John F. Kennedy
John Gay
John Glasworthy
John Habberton
John Joy Bell
John Kendrick Bangs
John Milton
John Philip Sousa
John Taintor Foote
Jonas Lauritz Idemil Lie
Jonathan Swift
Joseph A. Altsheler
Joseph Carey
Joseph Conrad
Joseph E. Badger Jr
Joseph Hergesheimer
Joseph Jacobs
Jules Vernes
Julian Hawthrone
Julie A Lippmann
Justin Huntly McCarthy
Kakuzo Okakura
Karle Wilson Baker
Kate Chopin
Kenneth Grahame
Kenneth McGaffey
Kate Langley Bosher
Kate Langley Bosher
Katherine Cecil Thurston
Katherine Stokes
L. A. Abbot
L. T. Meade

L. Frank Baum
Latta Griswold
Laura Dent Crane
Laura Lee Hope
Laurence Housman
Lawrence Beasley
Leo Tolstoy
Leonid Andreyev
Lewis Carroll
Lewis Sperry Chafer
Lilian Bell
Lloyd Osbourne
Louis Hughes
Louis Joseph Vance
Louis Tracy
Louisa May Alcott
Lucy Fitch Perkins
Lucy Maud Montgomery
Luther Benson
Lydia Miller Middleton
Lyndon Orr
M. Corvus
M. H. Adams
Margaret E. Sangster
Margret Howth
Margaret Vandercook
Margaret W. Hungerford
Margret Penrose
Maria Edgeworth
Maria Thompson Daviess
Mariano Azuela
Marion Polk Angellotti
Mark Overton
Mark Twain
Mary Austin
Mary Catherine Crowley
Mary Cole
Mary Hastings Bradley
Mary Roberts Rinehart
Mary Rowlandson
M. Wollstonecraft Shelley
Maud Lindsay
Max Beerbohm
Myra Kelly
Nathaniel Hawthrone
Nicolo Machiavelli
O. F. Walton
Oscar Wilde
Owen Johnson
P.G. Wodehouse
Paul and Mabel Thorne

Paul G. Tomlinson
Paul Severing
Percy Brebner
Percy Keese Fitzhugh
Peter B. Kyne
Plato
Quincy Allen
R. Derby Holmes
R. L. Stevenson
R. S. Ball
Rabindranath Tagore
Rahul Alvares
Ralph Bonehill
Ralph Henry Barbour
Ralph Victor
Ralph Waldo Emmerson
Rene Descartes
Ray Cummings
Rex Beach
Rex E. Beach
Richard Harding Davis
Richard Jefferies
Richard Le Gallienne
Robert Barr
Robert Frost
Robert Gordon Anderson
Robert L. Drake
Robert Lansing
Robert Lynd
Robert Michael Ballantyne
Robert W. Chambers
Rosa Nouchette Carey
Rudyard Kipling
Saint Augustine
Samuel B. Allison
Samuel Hopkins Adams
Sarah Bernhardt
Sarah C. Hallowell
Selma Lagerlof
Sherwood Anderson
Sigmund Freud
Standish O'Grady
Stanley Weyman
Stella Benson
Stella M. Francis
Stephen Crane
Stewart Edward White
Stijn Streuvels
Swami Abhedananda
Swami Parmananda
T. S. Ackland

T. S. Arthur
The Princess Der Ling
Thomas A. Janvier
Thomas A Kempis
Thomas Anderton
Thomas Bailey Aldrich
Thomas Bulfinch
Thomas De Quincey
Thomas Dixon
Thomas H. Huxley
Thomas Hardy
Thomas More
Thornton W. Burgess
U. S. Grant
Upton Sinclair
Valentine Williams
Various Authors
Vaughan Kester
Victor Appleton
Victor G. Durham
Victoria Cross
Virginia Woolf
Wadsworth Camp
Walter Camp
Walter Scott
Washington Irving
Wilbur Lawton
Wilkie Collins
Willa Cather
Willard F. Baker
William Dean Howells
William le Queux
W. Makepeace Thackeray
William W. Walter
William Shakespeare
Winston Churchill
Yei Theodora Ozaki
Yogi Ramacharaka
Young E. Allison
Zane Grey